THE JEW
AND HIS
HOME

THE JEW
AND HIS
HOME

By

ELIYAHU KITOV

Translated with an Introduction by

NATHAN BULMAN

EIGHTH EDITION

SHENGOLD PUBLISHERS, INC.
NEW YORK

Eighth Printing, 1976

ISBN: 0-88400-004-4

Library of Congress Catalog Card Number 63-17660

Published by Shengold Publishers, Inc., New York

Typography by G.M.T. Typographic Corp., New York

Printed in the United States of America

CONTENTS

A GUIDE TO OBSERVANCE

INTRODUCTION

There is widespread acknowledgement in the American Jewish community of a newly felt longing for the rediscovery of the sources of strength which have sustained our people in life from its earliest beginnings. The anxiety of our times presses for transformation into a new hope — one large enough to "rejoice us as we have been afflicted."

Many are the hopes for human betterment, which our times have proven illusory. Many the ideals in which we have reposed faith, which have been found wanting. Many are those who stand with renewed expectancy, with open ears for a new illumination of the Divine meaning which has accompanied our way of life as a people from time immemorial. But our generation can hear and understand Judaism's timeless teachings only if those teachings are addressed in its own idiom of language and experience. The truth and wisdom of Torah are beyond time; its channels of communication must be built — for us as for all previous generations — within time. On the other hand, we need equally to assure that in "pouring our old wine into new bottles," the wine should not be spoiled.

In the opinion of many, scholars and laymen, Eliyahu Kitov is one of the most gifted of the current builders of "bridges of communication," between the timeless wisdom of our heritage and the heart of this Jewish generation.

This book is the first comprehensive effort to build such a bridge of understanding in one of the most sensitive and vital areas of Jewish experience — the institution of the Jewish family. The Jewish family is the life cell of Jewish peoplehood. It is the point of meeting between the individual Jew and his people, between Israel's past and its future, between Divine Providence and Jewish history. On its strength, the physical and spiritual well-being of each Jewish person depends. On its strength, the ultimate well-being of the whole house of Israel depends.

To the task of conveying to our generation, the beautiful wisdom, the life-giving strength, the joyous holiness of the ideal Jewish family as projected in Jewish tradition, Eliyahu Kitov brings exceptional gifts of mind and heart. The author's Hebrew style is lyric, richly allusive, but sharply incisive. His point of view is unyieldingly rooted in classic Jewish tradition; while his sympathy for the difficulties of the contemporary Jewish situation is profound and moving. In Israel, the original Hebrew version of "The Jew And His Home," has been received with widespread and continuing acclaim. In translation Eliyahu Kitov's richly allusive Hebrew style poses considerable difficulties for English rendition. To the extent possible the translator strove to retain the flavor of the original, while seeking to conform to current English idiom.

In twenty-five chapters Kitov covers the entire range of concerns which comprise the life of the Jewish family. He describes the values of Jewish marriage and the character of the wedding ceremony. He continues with a loving treatment of such subjects as harmony in the home, the meaning and purpose of modesty, mutual esteem, loyalty and devotion, relations with relatives and neighbors. The author dwells broadly on conduct at meals, kashruth, the intimate aspects of Jewish family life, circumcision, the redemption of first-born sons, the upbringing of children and Bar Mitzvah. Many of the chapters are followed by sections containing accounts of Jewish law and customs in the subjects under discussion.

There emerges a composite picture of the noble structure of Jewish family life; a picture derived from the classical sources of Jewish tradition; one which faithfully reflects the ideal character of the Jewish family through our long existence.

My sincerest appreciation and thanks are extended to the author, Eliyahu Kitov, for his sustained and patient counsel and assistance, and his many marks of devoted friendship; to the publisher, Moshe Sheinbaum, President of Shengold Publishers, for his invaluable critical advice, his ever continual encouragement and unfailing cordiality; to my wife, for her faithful and devoted work in typing the manuscript, and her numerous critical suggestions.

May they all be rewarded by the inspiration which "The Jew And His Home" will engender in its readers; by the sacred happiness it will give to the families who will — with God's help — make of its ideals the pattern of their lives.

Tamuz, 5723   **Nathan Bulman**
June, 1963

ACKNOWLEDGMENTS

It is an extremely pleasant duty for me to record my heartfelt gratitude to the following individuals for their generous financial assistance towards the publication of the book.

RABBI SHALOM MIRKIN, Johannesburg, South Africa

SAMUEL C. FEUERSTEIN AND FAMILY, Brookline, Mass.

HERMAN TREISSER, New York, N. Y.

ABRAHAM TREGER, Jerusalem, Israel

ARIE CARMEL, London, England

ABRAHAM PARSHAN, Toronto, Canada

RABBI SHALOM KOVALSKY, Queens, N. Y.

DR. JOSEPH KAMINETSKY, Brooklyn, N. Y.

A. E. K.

FOREWORD TO THE ENGLISH EDITION

After the publication of the original Hebrew edition of "The Jew And His Home," I was approached by numerous rabbis, educators and laymen, who indicated to me the value and need of an English rendition of the book. They pointed out that no such work was available in the English language, that there were large numbers of potential readers in English speaking lands who eagerly seek the edification and knowledge which such a book as "The Jew And His Home" might give them. Initially, I was apprehensive that a faithful and adequate English rendition of "The Jew And His Home" might be difficult to achieve because of the particularities of its Hebrew idiom and style.

I was finally motivated in favor of undertaking the effort by the following considerations, which were urged upon me in numerous letters addressed to me, as well as to Israeli Religious Community Councils who have distributed the book to newly-wed couples. It was pointed out that on the one hand, the purely "religious" aspects of Jewish family life treated in the book, could be of much vital significance and enduring inspirational value to prospective readers; that on the other hand, "The Jew And His Home" discusses numerous themes of "universal" character and interest in the life of all families, whose illumination by the wise teachings of Jewish tradition could contribute much to enhancing the happiness of many a family.

Let it be noted that several previous efforts to translate "Ish Ubeito" (the book's Hebrew title) were begun, but were felt not to have been adequate in overcoming the previously noted difficulties. Very special thanks are therefore due to the present translator, Rabbi Nathan Bulman, who labored hard, and with noteworthy success, to remain faithful to the original both in content and style, while retaining felicitous English usage.

A particular note of thanks is due the publisher, Moshe Sheinbaum, President of Shengold Publishers, for his unstinting efforts in preparing the book for publication with utmost possible regard for aesthetic attractiveness. The interest he has exhibited, the marks of personal esteem and friendship he has shown me, his unfailing patience under often trying circumstance, his wise critical judgment, have all been extended far beyond the call of conventional obligation, and have elicited my heartfelt appreciation.

A final word of thanks is due to a devoted friend who first suggested this undertaking. Rabbi Shalom Mirkin of Johannesburg, South Africa, insistently expressed to the author his profound conviction of the prospective inspirational and educational value of "The Jew And His Home" for English speaking readers. A deeply felt sense of gratitude to him is hereby recorded.

Tamuz, 5723
June, 1963

A. Eliyahu Kitov

■ CHAPTER 1

■ KNOW YOUR HOME

■ In the midst of the material plenty of our time, many people are denied a sense of fulfillment in their lives — a fulfillment that in earlier days was the outcome of an awareness we seem to have lost. The awareness we refer to was of the vital significance of balance in life's intimate relations.

Lacking this sense of balance, people cannot contend with the powerful currents of life or enjoy the delights it has to offer. With it, they can walk the world with assurance, strong, happy, enjoying life in the confidence that they are living in harmony with the will of their Maker, certain of their ultimate well-being.

One man walks life's path with open eyes. Studying the signposts, he moves steadily toward his destination. He knows how to enjoy life's pleasures. He is not embittered by the necessary burdens he must carry, for he understands their purpose.

Another man goes blindly. Rushing after transient pleasures, he stumbles and falls. The pleasures that do not elude his grasp prove transitory, their seeming sweetness an illusion, their supposed benefit a peril.

Marriage is a crossroads on the map of life, perhaps the most vital decision a mature person ever has to make. Before entering on marriage, we must deliberate as to its meaning. We must

17

think through as carefully as we can what path to take that marriage may be a shining highway to happiness and fulfillment, rather than a blind alley ending in despair.

The home one wishes to build, the family whose roots one is planting — what do these signify? Knowing the answer to these basic questions, we will choose wisely at each of life's crossroads.

Our sages have much to teach us in this regard. The cumulative wisdom of ages can instruct us in how to read the meaning of time and life. This book summarizes the vital wisdom of traditional Jewish teaching.

CHAPTER 2

■ THE PRECIOUSNESS OF MARRIAGE

■ To understand the values of the Jewish home and family, one must first examine their foundation — Jewish marriage.

MARRIAGE IS OBLIGATORY

The Jewish view of marriage is a profoundly distinctive one.

We Jews do not regard marriage, as many religions do, as a matter of option, or unfortunately necessary concession, to nature's sensual demands, otherwise uncontrollable. We do not agree that total abstinence is the mark of saintliness.

Rather, Judaism views the married state as an *intrinsic good*, as *commandment* and *obligation*. Jewish tradition stringently prohibits abstinence from procreation. The only person who is exempt from this commandment is, in the words of Maimonides, one:

"whose soul incessantly yearns to study the Torah, who dwells in its confines with the singular concentration of Ben Azzai, who cleaves to the Torah all of his days. Only such a person is not considered sinful for abstaining from marriage."

19

THE ARTISAN KNOWS HIS VESSEL

Why do we affirm the value of the traditional Jewish view of marriage?

First let us remember that this view is drawn from the Torah; that its inner meaning has been defined and formulated by Jewish sages.

As in every area it covers, the Torah, as interpreted by our sages, is immutably fixed in reality. For He who created and fashioned us also gave us the Torah. He alone has perfect knowledge of His creatures; He alone knows what redounds to their benefit and what redounds to their injury. The Torah consists of the words addressed by the Divine Artisan to the human vessels He formed — His directions to the work of His hands.

Similarly we esteem the instructions of our sages because they are illuminated by the light of the Torah, even when not expressly stated in it or derived from the rules according to which the Torah may be interpreted. For, our sages' strength inheres not only in their profound reasoning and unerring logic; they have also penetrated the divine mystery and probed God's work — the soul of man.

Theirs is not investigation and knowledge from without. Rather, theirs is cognition and direct vision from within. It is as though they were partners in life's creative processes. The mystery of the universe, the soul's secrets, its every weakness — and how every weakness can be amended — all were an open book to them — the "book of man's generation."

Our sages have poured out their wisdom to us, that all men may find the way of life. We need but listen attentively to their words of wisdom and counsel. Let us listen to what they say about marriage.

PURE AS HEAVEN

Of the six hundred and thirteen commandments that God inscribed in his Torah, the commandment to procreate comes first. "Be fruitful and multiply" is the primary mitzvah.

On the third day of Creation the Creator commanded: "Let the earth put forth grass, herb yielding seed, and fruit-tree bearing fruit after its kind, wherein is the seed thereof, upon the earth."

On the fifth day after commanding "Let the waters swarm with swarms of living creatures, and let fowl fly above the earth in the open firmament of heaven," God blessed them, saying: "Be fruitful and multiply, and fill the waters in the sea, and let fowl multiply in the earth."

On the sixth day, He commanded: "Let the earth bring forth the living creature after its kind, cattle, and creeping thing, and beast of the earth after its kind." Finally, God created man in his own image. And to man, too, God said: "Be fruitful and multiply."

THE UNFINISHED TASKS OF CREATION

Man's desire for procreation derives from a pure source, from the will of the Creator, who desires that His work may endure.

"The world is built on benevolence." And the greatest kindness that the Creator has bestowed on His creatures is to leave His work unfinished — its completion is their task. In this act of creation they become their Master's constant associates. For God, never envying the work of His hands, has exalted man to an almost divine eminence. By giving man the capacity to rear progeny, He planted in man both the procreative impulse and a spontaneous love for every newborn infant — an innate readiness to protect and bring up their young till they, in turn, can make their own creative contribution to the continuous process of creation.

Hence the source of man's procreative impulse is pure and undefiled. Overflowing with grace, love, and compassion, it fills the world. And nowhere are these traits seen in greater beauty and perfection than in the relation of artist to his work, of parents to children.

Unfortunately, though matrimony was given to man as a blessing, he can turn it into a bitter curse — by failing to sanctify his marital relations.

How many lives have been shattered through the debasement of marital relations! How much distress has this caused the world!

For matrimony, which may be the greatest of blessings, may also be the worst of misfortunes. Which it will be depends on the character of the husband. If a man's soul is pure, his marriage will be pure. He will rejoice and take pride in his marriage, as in any genuine and beautiful achievement. But if his soul is sullied, he will be as ashamed of the marital act as he would of any personal failing.

IT IS NOT GOOD FOR MAN TO BE ALONE

It is not good for a man to be alone. Man should live in marriage with woman; he who repudiates the commandment to be fruitful associates with the evil in creation. Conversely, he who fulfills that commandment associates himself with the good of the world.

Our early sages said: "When the Torah admonished man not to violate the commandments lest 'thou serve thy enemy... in want of all things,' the reference was to 'want of a wife.'" (Nedarim 41).

It may seem to us that no one is "in want of all things" — but this saying of our sages teaches us that we who is unmarried really possesses nothing at all though it may not seem so to him.

For nothing that he possesses is his. What enjoyment can he derive from pleasures which must end with his own life? They are worthless even in the moment of possession.

But the good that the married man possesses is really his in the present, however much he may lack of temporal goods, and it will lead him to eternal life.

Our rabbis expatiated on this, declaring: "He who has no wife dwells without joy, without blessing, without good, without Torah, without protection, without peace." (Yebamoth 62)

"Without joy" — for only he whose path in the future is illuminated can have joy and he who dwells without a wife, looks towards a morrow which is already dark.

"Without blessing" — for only he who plants seed receives blessing — and he who dwells without a wife destroys his seed.

"Without good" — for only that is good which has consequences — and he who dwells without a wife cuts himself off from consequences.

"Without Torah" — for the essential purpose of Torah is to serve as an instrument for the building of new worlds, as it was God's instrument in the creation of His world — and he who dwells without a wife destroys his own world as well as that of his seed to come.

"Without protection" — for a man's best shield against the storms of life and the raging of his senses is his home. But he who dwells without a wife is exposed to every evil wind and every unchecked impulse, becoming as wind-beaten chaff.

"Without peace" — for only the man whose field is planted and produce blessed knows both inner and outer peace. And he who dwells without a wife sees the abodes of others filled with blessing, their children like olive saplings circling their tables, while his own inheritance is unblessed. How can peace dwell in *his* heart? His days are filled with agitation, with jealousy, with strife. He can never be at peace, with himself or with others.

"He who is unmarried is not fit to be called a man." Man was originally created whole. After the creation God removed a rib from Adam's side, making him incomplete. Fashioning Eve from Adam's side, He commanded that they cleave to one another — "And they shall be one flesh." When Adam and Eve discovered one another, they regained their original wholeness, and man was man again.

Hence God fashioned Eve from one of Adam's ribs, that their cleaving together might be a goodly thing, and an act of truth, that it might be impelled by nature; that they might be as branches drawing nourishment from a common stem, inseparable.

The cleaving together of man and woman is the very essence of their nature. He who remains unmarried is denying his own nature and loses the very name of man. He may seem a man, but is not one. The very name "man" in the holy tongue bespeaks an obligation to raise a family and to participate in Creation's continual process.

JEWISH CUSTOM

The people of Israel have made marriage an occasion for feasting and rejoicing. They rejoice in the awareness of the surpassing importance of marriage, the prime commandment. They exult in the knowledge that marriage is a gift bestowing joy and blessing, goodness and Torah, security and peace. They are happy in the consciousness that the marriage bond can bring their lives to perfection, restoring man to his original wholeness.

When Jews enter the covenant of marriage, they rejoice at having performed the mitzvah of their Maker's command. Their joy is doubled when they live to see their children married. And they fervently pray to be granted the joy of seeing children born to their sons and daughters.

Jewish parents, on the birth of a son or daughter, receive the blessing: May the newborn child "enter the portals of Torah, marriage, and good deeds."

The focus of concern of Jewish parents is preparation of their children for marriage. A generation or two ago a devout Jewish mother used to prepare her daughter's trousseau long in advance — sometimes from early infancy.

It used to be the Jewish custom for parents to enable their children to marry early, supplying their material needs until they were able to earn their own livelihood. To make this possible, many parents of small means willingly assumed onerous obligations. This is an indication of the sanctity that Judaism ascribed to marriage. For early marriage was regarded as a way of preventing wrongdoing, of removing temptation.

INSTRUCTION

But why was it necessary for the Torah to make marriage a religious obligation? Why did the sages think it necessary to enlarge on its merit and value? Would mankind not have married otherwise?

The answer to these questions is that it was the specific intent of the Torah and of the sages to instruct us in the sanctity of marriage. They wished explicitly to teach bride and groom that they were to view themselves as participants in the creation of a new world — a world of mitzvah and purity, of majesty and splendor, of blessing and peace. Marriage was not merely a matter of option and they wished bride and groom to be aware of this.

For the very awareness of the sublimity of a religious obligation exalts the person who is performing this obligation. It makes him upright in deed and trustworthy in speech. Since matrimony was given man in order to exalt him, the Torah wished to impress marriage's sanctity on him.

As our sages have said: "He who performs a religious obligation aware that it is such is superior to him who performs it unaware."

ESSENTIAL LAWS OF MARRIAGE

1. *Every person is commanded to marry for purposes of procreation, and whoever does not do so is as one who sheds blood. He diminishes the Divine in himself and causes the Divine Presence to depart from Israel.*

2. *From what age does the obligation apply? From the time one becomes eighteen years of age. And in any case one should not delay his marriage till after he is twenty. But a person who is engaged in the study of the Torah and is so engrossed in it that he fears that if married he will be caught up in financial burdens and will be distracted from his studies — such a person may delay his marriage; but he should not delay it too extensively.*

3. *Every man should seek to marry a respectable woman from a respectable family. There are three characteristics which are specific marks of Jewishness: shyness, kindness and good-heartedness. And whoever does not possess these characteristics is not worthy of being sought in marriage.*

4. *One may sell a scroll of the Torah in order to study Torah and in order to marry.*

5. *A Kohen is not permitted to marry a divorcee or a woman who has received Chalitza. He is not even allowed to remarry his own divorcee. An Israelite and Levite are permitted to remarry their own divorcees on condition that they did not marry other husbands in the meantime.*

6. *A woman who wishes to enter marriage after being widowed or divorced from her first husband must wait ninety days from the day she was widowed or divorced. The day she was divorced or widowed, and the day of her marriage do not count towards these ninety days.*

7. *If she is pregnant or nursing a child, she may not marry another man until the child is twenty-four months old.*

8. *Marriages are not performed on Sabbath or Festivals*

(nor on Chol Hamoed) nor on days of public mourning, such as most of the days of the counting of the Omer (between Passover and Shavuoth) or the period between the seventeenth day of Tammuz and Tisha B'Av; or during the week of mourning which follows the death of one of the nearest relatives of bride and bridegroom.

CHAPTER 3

■ THE CONSECRATION OF MARRIAGE

■ Our tradition teaches us how precious the obligation of matrimony is to Jews, and how high is the esteem of the person who fulfills it.

Jewish tradition says: "A groom is like a king."

"King Agrippa was wont to step aside for a bride," so that "she might wear her crown during her hour."

Our sages were not generally lavish with their praise, which they carefully weighed and measured. Why, then, did they compare a groom to a king? To teach us that he who takes a wife frees himself of the curse of being "in want of all things," and receives the blessing of "multitude of all things." In the same way, they said: "He who has found a wife has found goodness" — intimating that before marriage he had not known real "goodness." Only in marriage can a man receive this blessing — hence, he who takes a wife may be compared to a king.

Like a king, a bridegroom's every need is met.

Like a king, the groom is led to the marriage canopy to the accompaniment of music and dancing.

In a Jewish family, the father is king, the mother queen, the hour of their marriage the hour of coronation. For from that hour their entire lives are dedicated to the building of a miniature kingdom — a family.

The day on which husband and wife enter into the covenant of marriage may be compared to a Yom Kippur. Fasting, they return in penitence from the wrongdoing of their youth.

With marriage they erase all former guilt: previously, each had been but half a person, lacking peace and goodness. Now, with the hour of marriage they resume their original wholeness, again becoming one flesh. A new and a pure soul is again to be theirs, since their body is once again whole.

Bride and groom pray for forgiveness and atonement for the past. And the heavens grant their plea; their previous reckoning is erased, and a new one begins.

The hour when bride and groom stand under the *Chupah* resembles the hour of the closing prayer (*Neilah*), on the Day of Atonement (Yom Kippur). Their life's destiny is set. Gateways to heaven previously closed to them now open — and the hearts of bride and groom murmur in prayer: "Open Thou a new gate for us — as the old gate is closed."

Two benedictions are then recited. One is uttered over wine, for the hour is a joyous one, and "there is no joyous celebration without wine." The other is the benediction of betrothal, expressing praise and thanksgiving to Him who planted holiness in Jewish life, to Him who bade Israel abandon that which is prohibited and sanctify that which is prescribed.

Thus, the wedding canopy under which bride and groom stand as their lives are consecrated in the hour of marriage serves as a symbol of the holiness which is to pervade all of their lives as Jews. It is appropriate that the benediction reads: "Blessed art Thou, O Lord, who sanctifies His people Israel through bridal canopy and consecration."

When the first two benedictions have been made, the groom places a ring on the bride's finger and says: "Behold thou art consecrated to me with this ring, in accordance with the law of Moses and Israel."

Which is to say: As the law of Moses and Israel is of divine origin and bears the seal of truth, so shall our marriage be consecrated by divine holiness and truth. And as the law of Moses and Israel forever consecrates all those who enter its covenant, so shall we be consecrated forever.

The groom *does not* say: "Thou art wed to me, bound to me, acquired by me." He says only: "Thou art consecrated to me." No thing that is consecrated for a sacred purpose may be profaned — and from the moment of marriage, the bride is forbidden to all other men. From that moment bride and groom begin a life to be governed entirely by the rule of holiness — the law of Moses and Israel.

In the Torah and the prophetic writings the term *Erusin*, meaning "betrothal," is used to designate the act of *Kidushin*, "consecration by marriage"; Israel's prophets used the same term, *Erusin*, as a symbol of the covenant between God and Israel. Their description of the conditions of that covenant helps us to understand the intent of Jewish marriage.

In a parable, the prophet Hosea makes Israel's betrothal by God dependent on seven conditions, six of which apply to God, as it were, one to Israel.

"And I will betroth thee unto Me for ever;

"Yea, I will betroth thee unto Me in righteousness, and in justice.

"And in lovingkindness, and in compassion.

"And I will betroth thee unto Me in faithfulness;

"And thou shalt know the Lord."

The same seven conditions apply to the betrothal of husband and wife. Six are the husband's responsibility, one is the wife's.

"For ever" — a husband may not, while consecrating his wife, entertain the thought of divorce.

"In righteousness" — a husband may not bring up false charges against his wife, to justify his desire to break the marriage bond.

"In justice" — even if his wife wrongs him, the husband may not treat her unjustly.

"In lovingkindness" — the husband must always act compassionately, rather than rigorously, toward his wife.

"And in faithfulness" — the husband dare not simulate affection for his wife when his heart belongs to another.

These are the six conditions of betrothal that the husband assumes. The wife, for her part, assumes one stipulation. This, if heeded, renders her consecration one of truth, her betrothal free of deceit: "And thou shalt know the Lord."

A wife has no need of the admonitions addressed to her husband, her very nature assuring her loyalty. Similarly, the traits of compassion and righteousness are more deeply rooted in her being.

But in one respect the wife needs to be admonished more than her husband — her reverence for her husband must not exceed her reverence for God. Were it not for the "fear of sin" especially enjoined on the wife, the home might collapse. For man is more sensual than woman; when his senses are aroused, he is capable of overturning the foundations of the home — sanctity and purity. At such moments, the wife is capable of restraining her husband's raging impulses. Properly guarded and applied, this capacity of the wife's can strengthen and preserve the Jewish home.

Hence: "Thou shalt know the Lord" is primarily addressed to woman.

When a Jewish husband and wife are consecrated to one another, they are taught how to assure a marriage that will always be one of truth and eternity, of righteousness and compassion, of the knowledge and fear of God.

THE KETHUBAH (MARRIAGE CONTRACT)

When the groom has finished reciting the formula of consecration, the marriage contract is read. The *Kethubah* is a legally binding document of confidence and trust which lists the husband's obligations to his wife. The *Kethubah's* stipulations, additions, even the phrasing of the text — all are of great antiquity. Its basic aim is to strengthen and affirm the wife's dignified status, as well as to confer a number of special rights and privileges on her. These serve to deter the husband from severing the marital bonds with arbitrary ease, indifferent to his wife's subsequent well-being.

When the *Kethubah* was instituted among Jews, the Gentiles still viewed the woman as an object of possession. A wife was considered her husband's servant. The sages, in enacting the *Kethubah*, marked the esteem in which the Jewish wife was to be held.

She was not to be viewed as some religions did, as a "daughter of Satan," but as the heart and soul of the home, not as a source of defilement, but as a source of the home's purity and sanctity.

In the words of the sages: "A man is obliged to love his wife as himself, and to honor her *more than himself.*"

After the *Kethubah* has been read, properly witnessed and signed, the seven benedictions of marriage are recited.

The first is recited over wine, for, as we have noted, "there is no rejoicing without wine."

The second benediction recalls the creation of the world. For bride and groom, it is as though marriage is a renewal of the world.

The third benediction alludes to the fashioning of man — the newly-weds are as reborn.

The fourth benediction celebrates the act of Divine Providence in mating the bridal pair and bringing them together.

The fifth affirms faith in God's eventual restoration of Zion and Jerusalem. For the memory and hope of Zion takes precedence over every joy, however great.

The sixth benediction gives thanks for the personal joy of bride and groom. It contains the prayer that their rejoicing might be perfect — that, as there was no encroachment on the perfect faithfulness of Adam and Eve, who were alone in the world, so might there be no encroachment on the love of the bride and groom.

The seventh and final benediction is a paean of praise to the Lord for having sweetened all of human life through the happiness granted bride and groom, and for having granted mankind the supreme gift of love and brotherhood, peace and friendship.

THE FIRST WEDDING

This is how our rabbis envisioned the first wedding:

When the Holy One, Blessed be He, created Eve, He made her lovely and built canopies for her that were decked with gold and jewels. Himself He led her to the *Chupah*, Himself He entertained bride and groom, that they might rejoice. He bade His angels do the same, and they danced, played, and sang for Adam and Eve. The angels presented the first bride and groom with gifts of all that was most precious in the world. And God in His glory uttered the marriage benedictions over them.

Whenever a man and woman enter marriage in purity to build a pure Jewish home, the Divine Presence rests on their *Chupah*. The heavenly angels descend to rejoice with them; to the benediction addressed to bride and groom, the angels cry, "Amen! May it be God's will!"

■ ESSENTIAL OBSERVANCES ON THE WEDDING DAY

1. *It is customary for bride and groom to fast on their wedding-day, since marriage should be approached soberly and earnestly. (Another reason for the fast is that their sins are forgiven on that day). Hence they should dedicate the day to prayer to God that His Divine Presence may always rest upon them.*

2. *The bride and groom add "Aneinu" (Answer us ...") to their Mincha prayers, as is done on a regular fast day, and their fast should continue till after the wedding. If the ceremony takes place at night, they may eat something after nightfall.*

3. *If their wedding-day falls on Rosh Chodesh (New moon) or the day after the festival of Weeks (Shavuot) or on the 15th of Av or the 15th of Shevat, or on Chanuka or Shushan Purim, they do not fast. But on the 1st of Nissan and of Ellul, it is customary to fast in spite of Rosh Chodesh.*

4. *The marriage ceremony is performed in the presence of ten Jewish men by an authorized Rabbi, or expert in marriage-law, and in the presence of two admissible witnesses, who are not related to bride and groom.*

5. *It is customary for the groom to shatter a glass vessel immediately after the wedding ceremony, to recall our grief at the destruction of Jerusalem, as is written in the verse "If I set not Jerusalem above my chiefest joy."*

6. *Immediately after the ceremony, bride and groom are led to a private room in order that they may have some privacy for a short while. Their entry to this room should be observed by two witnesses.*

7. *A man may not reside with his wife even briefly without a Kethuba. Thus care should be taken that the Kethuba*

be entrusted to the bride or her relatives immediately after the ceremony for safe keeping. If the Kethuba is at any time lost, a Rabbi should immediately be approached in order to draw up a new document.

ENGLISH TRANSLATION OF THE STANDARD TEXT OF THE KETHUBA

On the .... day of the week, the............... day of the month of............... of the year............... after the creation of the world, (corresponding to the............... day of the month of..............., of the year...............) according to the date as recorded in this city...............

We witness here that............... son of............... spoke to............... daughter of............... and said: Be thou my wife according to the law of Moses and of Israel, I promise to work for thee, honor thee, nourish thee and support thee, as is the manner of Jewish men who work for, honor, nourish and support their wives.

And I shall give thee the dowry of thy maidenhood, two hundred pieces of silver (according to the value of...............) to which thou art entitled by the law of the Torah, as also thy food, clothing and all thy needs, and will be with thee, as is the way of the world.

And the said maiden............... consented to become his wife. And this is the dowry which she has brought to him from the home of her parents, be it in silver, gold, jewelry, clothing, and bedding, a total of...............

And the said groom............... willingly added to this a third, an amount of..............., making a total of...............

And the said groom............... willingly added a further amount of............... making a total of...............

And this is what the groom............... said: The responsibility for this contract and the additions thereto, and the dowry and the additions thereto, I take upon myself and upon my heirs after me, to be collected from the best and choicest of my properties and of any possession which I may have anywhere already, or which I may acquire in the future, whether of movable or immovable property; all shall serve as warranty and as security from which this marriage contract and the additions thereto may be collected, and even the garment on my shoulders will be a security for such a collection whether I am alive or dead, from this day unto eternity.

And the said groom............... accepted the responsibility for this marriage contract and the additions thereto, to be valid as are all contracts of marriage and the additions thereto which are customary for Jewish women, and are drawn up according to the enactment of our sages of blessed memory — not as a mere token and formality.

And we have received a mark of acquisition thereunto from the said groom............... to............... his bride, regarding all that has been written and enumerated above, in receiving from him an article suitable to serve as a token, and all the above is thus valid and in force.

CHAPTER 4

■ WHERE JOY DWELLS

■ Though a man live in the most palatial of residences, he will not have founded a home until he takes a wife. As Israel's wise sages said: "A man's wife is his home."

A man's concerns and work take him away from home. A woman's concern is directed inward, toward the home. It is she who manages the household. Though a man succeeds on the outside, true satisfaction and repose awaits him only at home.

REST AND JOY AT HOME

Man and woman differ in understanding and insight as they do in nature. Men acquire understanding largely through social intercourse — men who are restricted to the confines of their homes have but a narrow understanding. But women find their insight largely within themselves. Indeed, insights that are communicated to them from abroad often impair their natural insight. The difference is one between wisdom and insight. Wisdom derives from communication, insight flows from the self. In depth of insight, in intuition, the rabbis considered woman superior to man.

Hence, that home is unfortunate where the husband continually draws his wife into the vortex of his outside business, into his agitated life outside the home. For life's raging currents invade that home, and there is no escaping the strife of the outside world.

That husband and wife are fortunate who realize that neither is suited to perform the other's functions, and that the separate endeavors enjoyed by their different natures can yield a harvest of happiness for both of them. And home is the only place where they can reap that harvest.

THE SEVEN DAYS OF REJOICING

Now that the newlyweds have made a home, they are to fill it with joy. For the seven days after the *Chupah*, the husband is to leave off his work and business. He is to be free to enjoy his home for one complete week. All else is to be secondary to the joy of bride and groom in one another. They need not go away in quest of that joy. It is in their own home. And there is enough joy for them to share it with others. Every new guest during these seven festive days renews their rejoicing. After every meal where a new guest is entertained, the seven 'marriage benedictions are again recited, as under the *Chupah*.

Bride and groom may celebrate the seven festive days in their own home, indicating that there is where their future joy will be found.

The practice of traveling for a month of honeymoon is not praiseworthy, for travel, at its most pleasant, is a tiring and unsettling affair, and diminishes the bride and groom's real happiness.

Perhaps the point of the honeymoon is to distract bride and groom from a very difficult period of transition, until the adjustment is made. But Jews find holiness and sublimity in marriage, and have no need of such a distraction. A Jewish bride and groom can do no better than to rejoice in their own home, in rest and tranquility, and in genuine happiness.

CHAPTER 5

■ "AND I WILL DWELL IN THEIR MIDST"

■ Some of our sages probe not only the words of the Torah, but each individual letter as well. The foremost exponent of this method was Rabbi Akiba. It was he who taught:

"If husband and wife are deserving, God's Presence dwells in their midst. If they are not deserving, fire devours them."

"For," said Rabbi Akiba, "the Hebrew word for man is *ish*, spelled *aleph, yod, shin*. Remove the *yod*, and you have *aleph shin*, or *esh*, meaning fire. The Hebrew word for woman is *ishah*, spelled *aleph, shin heh*. Remove the *heh* and, once again, you have *esh*, meaning "fire.""

From this we learn that there is a consuming fire in the heart of every man and woman. When they marry, two fires are brought together that are capable of destroying whole worlds, if not properly tended. To quench that fire is impossible — for it generates the life of the world. But to leave the fire as it is is also impossible, for it generates evil as well.

What did God do? He placed one of the letters of His name, the first letter of the Divine Name, *yod*, between the *aleph* and the *shin* to make the Hebrew name for "man." And he took the second letter of His Name, the *heh*, and placed it after the *aleph* and the *shin* to make the Hebrew name for "woman." In that way, both man and woman retain in their names the word "fire," but when they marry, the Divine Presence dwells in their midst, in the combination of their names.

Wherever God's presence dwells, that fire gives warmth and heat, but it does not devour and consume. If husband and wife do not make the Divine Presence unwelcome, its blessing rests on the work of their hands and they become as partners in the act of Divine creation. But if they make the Presence unwelcome so that it does not dwell in their midst, they are left only with two consuming flames.

Every Jewish home is intended as a sanctuary in little. Those who dwell in it are to be as priests, the functions that take place in it are as a sacred altar service.

The offerings of that sacred service are: control of the profane fire in the hearts of husband and wife; avoidance of quarrels; mutual lovingkindness and support; employment of nature's flame only as permitted, in fulfillment of divine commandment and to maintain the world; the rearing of generations sanctified from birth; and a loving willingness to bear the burdens of home — be they of child-rearing, of neighborliness, of charity.

No offerings are as dear to God as these. Homes where such offerings are consistently made are in truth sanctuaries, from which he who will lead Israel to salvation may emerge.

— — — — — — — — — — — —

"How goodly are thy tents, O Jacob, thy tabernacles, O Israel!"

The children of Israel built dwelling places for God in many places that His Presence might rest among them: in the wilderness, in Gilgal, in Shiloh, in Nob, Gibeon, and Jerusalem. Wherever His name was mentioned, God came down and blessed that place. God said: "I shall leave all of My heavenly legions and descend to dwell among Israel."

Now, though all those dwelling places are in ruins, as is His holy temple where He chose to dwell, there is one dwelling place of God which can never be destroyed — a Jewish home. In that home the divine service continues uninterrupted; the Jewish family will be the source of the redemption of Israel.

It has been said: "If you wish to understand the people of Israel, acquaint yourself with a Jewish family. Even if that people should be completely destroyed, it can still be rebuilt from the last surviving family."

On what basis? On the strength of the divine promise: "I shall dwell in their midst" — the promise made to every Jewish family.

CHAPTER 6

■ DOMESTIC BLISS (SHALOM BAYIT)

■ A Jewish home may be distinguished by a number of characteristics having to do with religious observance and ethical practices. These practices are numerous: some call for daily observance, others are required only on special occasions. Some practices concern relations between husband and wife; others concern relations between the couple and other persons, their Maker, their children. Some practices are confined to the home; others extend beyond. No one volume can comprehensively treat them all. We shall touch only on those practices in the Jewish home which are fundamental for the entire prescribed pattern of behavior.

The traditional Hebrew phrase for domestic bliss is *Shalom Bayit*, meaning "a peaceful home." Let us begin with the concept of peace.

THE TRUE TEST OF SHALOM

People vary widely in their attitude toward *Shalom.* There are those who are always quarreling, with both relatives and strangers. They are the most blameworthy. At the opposite pole are those praiseworthy persons who are always at peace with everyone.

39

Between these two extremes people fall into two categories: those who get along with strangers, but not with friends and relatives, and vice versa. The behavior of those who are at peace with their friends and relatives, but not with strangers, is a first step on the way to true peace.

The person who is friendly with strangers has not yet passed the test of *Shalom*. For he may be motivated by praise or self-interest. Perhaps he can be friendly disposed to the stranger simply because of infrequent contact with him. At home, the same person may flare up at the slightest provocation.

Home is the true test of *Shalom*. The person who can keep his temper under control at home really is dominated by the desire for *Shalom*. If he were not, his self-restraint would soon snap under the constant friction of family life. Why can't he get along as well with strangers? Because the trait of *Shalom* is not strong enough in his character as a whole. But if he really wished and worked at it, there is the strong probability that he could achieve an attitude of friendliness toward *all* people. He need only understand that all men are brothers, and *Shalom* applies to them as well as to his kith and kin.

SHALOM NOT AN IDYLLIC STATE

Shalom is not an idyllic state. Two people may be completely compatible, love one another spontaneously, and enjoy an idyllic relationship, yet they may not live in a relationship of *Shalom*. For *Shalom* was not meant only for the lucky inhabitants of Paradise. Ordinary mortals are expected to live in *Shalom*, run-of-the-mill people incapable of sustaining an idyllic state. The paradox is that true *Shalom* is to be found where people differ in fundamental respects — in behavior, in aspirations, in desires — where love is not quite pure, and anger presses for expression. That is the true test of *Shalom*.

The person who really loves *Shalom*, pursues it. Under extreme provocation he will say to himself: "Come what may, I won't quarrel. I *will* keep the peace. For nothing is worse than quarreling."

"Who maketh peace in his high places" — reads the passage. Our sages said: "An angel of fire and an angel of water stand side by side and do one another no harm. For God has put one desire in both their hearts: to stand before and serve Him who created both fire and water."

AT HOME

He who truly loves *Shalom*, must know the obstacles in its way and how to overcome them.

It is hard to keep peace everywhere, but it is hardest of all to do so at home. It is not too difficult to flee conflict with the world — one can always escape to his home. But it is terribly hard to escape the effects of conflict within the walls of one's home. There is simply no refuge.

Mordecai the Just was head of the Sanhedrin — the highest rabbinic tribunal. "Greatest of the Jews," second only to the king, "universally respected, a lover of his people" — but the account of Mordecai the Just's praises reaches its apex with the last descriptive phrase: he "spoke peace for all his children."

"All his children" — the phrase is pregnant with meaning. A man may have the obedience of one son, but not of another, of one grandchild, but not of another. Those who obey him he loves; to them he "speaks peace." But Mordecai the Just "spoke peace to all his children," obedient or not. Scripture, in making Mordecai the Just's pursuit of peace at home the culmination of his virtues, interprets it as superior even to his seeking peace for his people.

The fact is that no man is quarrelsome at home without cause. But what is the gain from quarreling? One small fault may have been corrected, only to be replaced by a greater one. For nothing is more hateful to God and more harmful to people than strife.

Admittedly, every one is obligated to prevent misbehavior at home. But banishing strife is an even more important obligation. If one can accomplish both, well and good. If not, *Shalom* takes precedence.

The man who sacrifices peace to some other goal, however important, for the most part ends up by accomplishing nothing, except to make his home an inferno. He will have turned it into a scene of contention among all the members of his household, himself included. Once the flame of controversy is lit, it will keep burning. He will not have saved those values for which he fought; what he still possessed, *Shalom Bayit*, he will have lost. On the other hand, if he gives *Shalom Bayit* priority, it will prevent, or repair any breach in the walls of his home. When there is love at home, admonitions are obeyed.

CAUSES OF DISSENSION

Men naturally consider themselves masters of their homes.

They wish the respectful attention of the members of their household to their needs, whether expressed or not.

This attitude does not derive from the old days, when men fought for their women. Nor is it the result of social convention, of habit, or of meanness of spirit. It is a law of nature, which the Creator implanted in His creatures, for their good. For home and family are like a kingdom in little, to be ruled only by one king. The wife is the queen of beauty, of love, and compassion — royalty is the crown that sits on the husband's head. He who seeks to alter that law of nature endangers his own welfare and harms his family. The laws of nature are not to be changed. If not properly understood, man's need to be master of his own household can be a threat to Shalom Bayit.

If the members of the household demonstrate by their behavior that they have no concern with the wishes and opinions of the head of the family; if they go so far as to disobey his express desires; if they deliberately spite him; if they completely ignore his wishes, as though he were non-existent — the head of the family is apt to try to impose his will on them by force. A home in such a state of war is in dire straits. As our sages said: "A home where there is dissension will not stand." (Derech Eretz Zuta 9).

Whoever "wins" this war, both parties lose. If "they" are the winners, the home loses its dignity. If "he" succeeds in imposing his mastery, he may have saved his crown, but he has lost his kingdom — there is a growing abyss between the head and the rest of the household. If neither side triumphs, and the war continues, the home will become a veritable living hell.

Let us consider possible situations.

A man's income is not sufficient for expensive living. Or his income is sufficient, but years of economizing have left him stingy. Or a man is open-handed and generous by nature, while the members of his household tend to scrimp. Or a man has more than enough money, but is niggardly.

Or a man has modest tastes, and prefers his home to be quiet and calm, while his family prefers the immodesty of neighbors — as expressed in word, dress, and conduct. Or the opposite may be true.

Or a man may have a clear conception of the way of life he should like to follow. He may try to persuade his family to accept that way of life, which is associated with his character and philosophy — only to have them reject it.

42

Or a man may be completely immersed in his own outside affairs, and completely indifferent to those of his family. He may consider his family's interests as trivial, and resent their involvement in them. What he may resent even more may be the family's efforts to make *him* part of their triviality, imposing their do's and dont's on him in the family relationship.

Or a man may expend all his energy in pursuit of a living — only to come home exhausted and have his wife insist that he perform a chore that properly belongs to her, one that he is either incapable or unwilling to perform.

Or a man may have an introspective nature, keeping many of his concerns from his own wife. Or he may find it easy to talk of his worries to others, but not to the members of his own family. His family cannot accept this exclusion from the confidence of the head of the household. They see it as an evidence of his lack of regard for them. But he cannot change his nature. Their constant criticism angers him — and he feels himself driven to the limit of his endurance by their constant carping and nagging.

Now a man is constantly involved in social associations. He is always talking, listening, joining in activities with other people, whether he likes to or not. His whole body — mouth, ears, nerves — are charged and tense all day. He longs for the moment when he can return home and escape the incessant talking and noise. But his wife has been busy all day at home alone. She has been waiting all day for her husband to come home, so she will have someone to talk to. At the end of the day they are both disappointed. He does not wish to talk, or she to be silent. Before they know it, they are quarreling bitterly.

ESCAPING DISSENSION

All these situations endanger *Shalom Bayit*. How can one escape that danger?

The head of the household must begin by establishing self-control over his temper. Once he has gained that control, he will gain discipline. The members of his household will try to please him of their own free will.

A man will sacrifice anything for the esteem of the world. No effort is too dear for him, to secure such esteem. It should be no more difficult for him to achieve any other desired end. In most instances, one cannot be sure of the value of one's efforts — but there is no doubting the value of self-control. The psychologists say that self-control is the secret of happiness.

But a person must get angry sometimes! The thing to do when one is angry is to do something to lower one's "temperature" immediately — by going to sleep, by diverting the anger to some other object, by leaving the home for a while. A person ought never to expend the force of his anger on his home.

But a person can't always approve of what goes on at home! True, more things happen at home to drive a person to impatience and danger than happen anywhere else. But one must always try to weigh the dubious advantages of anger against the certain advantages of self-restraint. A person who gets in the habit of making this calculation will eventually find the strength in himself to control his temper. For he will put in one scale of the balance the vexation his wife and family may cause him; in the other scale he will put the unease and pain that dissension brings, its destructiveness of home life. Which is the greater sorrow, the heavier anguish? Obviously, dissension.

The peace-loving man concludes: "Even when I think I have cause, I must not answer strife with strife. Otherwise, there will be no *Shalom Bayit* — the peace that relieves all other pressures of life."

Your wife is demanding. She presses you for the money you do not have. Or she is extravagant and squanders the money you do have. She is close-fisted when it comes to spending money on household necessities. She is inhospitable and uncharitable. She is loud. She is a gadabout, forever away from home. Or else she is forever bringing neighbors into her home. Or vice versa — nobody is welcome in her home, and she never goes anywhere. She is forever nagging you over trivial matters; she insists you do her chores. Or she is always suspicious of you. Your children are disobedient.

How are you to respond?

You must not abandon your responsibilities as the head of the family. Do not turn away from them in resentment. Listen to what your wife and children have to say. Perhaps your judgment is not completely justified. You may discover that you are at fault, when you lend an ear to the words of those who, in the last analysis, are your nearest and dearest, bone of your bone and flesh of your flesh. You may share some of the responsibility for your misery.

If you are sensible of your own faults and wish to be obeyed, do not be stubborn. Admit the truth, confess that you may have been wrong. That will not lower you in their esteem. To the contrary: He who admits the truth gains stature in the eyes of others. This is particularly true in cases where the admission seems attended by self-deprecation.

SELF-STUDY

Everything God created was created perfect. Nothing was created without purpose. Difference and contradiction, too, are the handiwork of the Creator, created for the perfecting of the world. Thus, there are many states of nature necessary for the world's continued existence which are exclusive of one another. Fire and water, dry land and sea, are mutually exclusive. But God did not say of the state of exclusiveness and contradiction that "it is good" — the judgment He made of the rest of Creation. All the more so, is it true of the state of human strife and dissension, that the best of intentions cannot smooth them over. No man can claim purity of motivation. Strife and dissension are bad, even where the person responsible for them believes himself to be completely in the right. On the other hand, it is the law of nature that a man should be the master of his home; to establish that role is to contribute to the advancement of life. However, the person who wishes to consolidate his role as master of his home through strife and quarreling must be quite sure that his zeal is completely free of any taint of selfish pleasure or dictatorial tendency. Thus motivated, he is bound to lose the love of his dear ones, bound to arouse their hostility and antagonism. That is why a man must study himself very carefully for possible error.

The same holds true of the other traits and opinions in which a man may differ from the members of his household. No one is so righteous that his motives and character are beyond reproach, so that those who differ from him are always at fault. People are too close to themselves to see their faults clearly — but others do see them.

A man should attempt to judge dispassionately those differences between himself and his household which flow from differences of circumstance. Not every person can rise above the routine of his life. It is the way of the world for a person to consider his own activities important, those of others less so; to see his own efforts as difficult, those of others as easy. No differences that spring up between husband and wife on this question can justify a quarrel. Obviously, neither side in the dispute can be completely right. The truth lies somewhere between the two extremes.

A man has the right to rest both physically and mentally when he returns home from a hard day's work. But a woman has the right to see a smile on her husband's face, to hear loving words from him after she has been waiting for him all day to return home. If husband and wife are impatient with one another, and cannot meet one another's need — both are at fault, and neither has the right to complain. Both lack understanding and patience with one another.

Though both are at fault, more may be demanded of the husband than of the wife in the way of a special effort to achieve insight into his wife's feelings and thoughts. For a man is more open by temperament and character; to understand a woman requires special pains. Men are tougher, more resistant to trouble. Women, on the other hand, being gentler, are more easily moved to tears. Attracted to beauty, women love harmony and order more than do men. They are more deeply affected by coarseness and disharmony. The wife consequently is more easily disturbed by the loss of peace of mind.

There is one general principle for ensuring family happiness. Such happiness does not depend on similarities in temperament and character between husband and wife, but on the harmonization of their individual differences. The ideal is a mutual enrichment out of respect for one another — specifically in those areas where they differ.

If a husband does not confide his affairs to his wife, they are quite likely to exchange sharp words. Were the husband to plumb his wife's personality, he would understand why she considers this secretiveness an insult. What place is there for secrecy between two people who are sworn to a covenant of eternal truth? The wife naturally suspects that her husband is not being honest with her; either he does not trust or he does not respect her.

On the other hand, were the wife to fathom her husband's character, she could find a reason for his behavior, and attribute it not to lack of confidence or disrespect but to other causes.

She might deduce that he is troubled over some affair or other, or oversensitive to some weakness of his own. Hence he has found it difficult to discuss what was troubling him calmly, or has hesitated to reveal his weakness. As a result, he was trying to distract himself from a too-heavy burden by not talking about it. When he feels a momentary need to unburden himself, he might prefer to do so with a stranger, who would soon turn to other concerns of his own. But his wife, once involved in her husband's cares, might constantly dwell on them, repeatedly seeking to engage him in conversations he would rather avoid. A husband might prefer not to reveal his cares to his wife for still another reason. In speaking to relative strangers, he could tell them only part of what was disturbing him. Most often, his problems were the product of his own weakness; should he tell them at length, he would be revealing his weakness completely. He is too sensitive for that. But, in speaking to a stranger, he could manage to slip into the story of his difficulties, details favorable to himself to balance out the discreditable elements in his story. After all, the stranger does not know him well.

But a husband could never do that with his wife. If he should reveal but part of his troubles to her, she would immediately guess the rest, and he would lose her respect. Even if there were mitigating circumstances that he could cite in self-justification, he might hesitate to do so, suspecting that it might sound to her like extravagant self-praise. So he prefers to conceal his troubles from her.

Husband and wife, being close and loving friends, should ideally know each other, seek to harmonize their character differences, and giving another the benefit of the doubt, avoid quarrels. But not every husband and wife are thus fortunate. At times their knowledge may not help. Or, they may try to give one another the benefit of the doubt, but be unable to control their anger. And anger, once let loose, makes it impossible to distinguish the proper from the improper reaction. All the same, it is better to be angry and contrite than to justify the anger by insisting that it is right. Before reacting with anger to any situation at home, one ought to try to analyze the possible causes for the conflict — particularly one's own possible responsibility — it may turn out that one is not oneself completely free of the same fault one finds in one's relations! Till then, practice restraint even where you think yourself justified in losing your temper.

HOW TO REACT

When you see something improper or shameful happening at home that requires criticism or protest — either to prevent its recurrence, or not to lend it your tacit consent — you have the right to register criticism — but only when you are certain that you have no ulterior motives, and that your action will have positive rather than negative consequences.

There are many ways of reacting: with violence, scolding, harsh looks, reproaches, explanations, pleading, angry or sorrowful silence. There is a time and a place for each method. It is hard to formulate one general principle to cover all situations, but some specific generalizations are possible. Some of the methods may be useful on certain occasions, other methods on different occasions. Some may be fraught with no danger, others with great danger.

Violence, scolding, and harsh looks are the strongest measures. In most cases and for most people they are not efficacious, and they are far too dangerous. Scolding requires a precise knowledge of just how severe one's words ought to be and how they are likely to affect the person being scolded.

The wisest course of action is to be quiet at the moment of anger or anguish. Such a silence, accompanied by the strained suffering that shows itself on one's face, makes an indelible impression on those who love one, and is more effective than a thousand remonstrations. When anger has passed, that is the time for mild reproach, made at an appropriate occasion when people feel love for one another again. Silence at the moment and reproach later form a wise reaction pattern.

True, this is very hard, and one cannot always do it. But people go through harder crises. Earning a living is hard, and bringing up children is even harder. Getting along with people in society is hard, too; one's obligations to one's country and state are harder still. Still, no one ever throws up his hands in despair at the prospect of earning a living or meeting his social obligations. It's a matter of try, and try again.

Don't be disheartened by the difficulties involved in maintaining *Shalom Bayit*. Just determine to behave as you know you should. Consider every test of your determination as though it were unique, never to be repeated. Say to yourself you have only one test to pass, and even the weakest-willed person can pass one test. As Jewish tradition puts it, God helps him who passes one test to pass a second. The third will be still easier — "and a threefold cord is not quickly broken."

There are a number of hedges one can put up against giving vent to anger. What line to draw depends on the individual. One scholar was said to have had a special garment that he put on when he grew angry. He said, "I won't let myself be angry until I have put on this garment." That was his hedge. In other words, he could not always control his anger, but he could always delay it. Meanwhile, the intensity of his anger would subside.

A person who can control his anger in this fashion will eventually achieve *Shalom Bayit*. He will certainly be master of his own home. He will be heeded, and need fear no sudden storm or terror. The home that is built on the foundations of truth and peace can serve as a nation's foundations.

THE LIGHTS OF PEACE

The concept of peace is the most beloved among Jews. People greet each other in the market place with "Shalom." The final benediction of the prayer service concludes with a prayer for peace. The priestly blessing ends with peace. Abraham was promised: "Thou shalt go to thy fathers in peace." The patriarch Jacob asked only: "So that I come back to my father's house in peace." God praised Aaron the priest: "My covenant was with him of life and peace." For his zeal Phineas was rewarded with: "Behold I give unto him my covenant of peace." The Torah is identified with peace: "And all her paths are peace." God himself is called "the Lord of peace." The Holy One, Blessed be He, will console Jerusalem with peace: "And my people shall abide in a peaceable habitation." To punish Ammon and Moab, He withheld peace from them: "Thou shalt not seek their peace nor their prosperity." Even in time of war the children of Israel were commanded to seek peace: "When thou drawest nigh unto a city to fight against it, then proclaim peace unto it."

Israel's sages cherished peace so highly that in its name they lit a lantern which they set in every Jewish home to illuminate it with the light of peace.

When the Hasmoneans emerged victorious over their Hellenistic oppressors, they purified the sanctuary of the Lord and restored the crowns of priesthood and of sovereignty to Israel. To commemorate the miracle of the jar of oil that burned for eight days though it held enough oil to burn only one day, our sages ordained that lights be kindled in Jewish homes during the eight days of Chanukah. The light of Chanukah was a light of deliverance, of holiness, of sovereignty. It needs to be kindled only eight days during the year. But the Sabbath lights are kindled every week throughout the year. For the Sabbath light is the light of the peace of the Jewish home. Israel's sages sought to make sure that *Shalom* would reign in Jewish homes — hence they ordained the kindling of the Sabbath candles at the advent of each Sabbath — lights of peace for the Sabbath of peace.

The Chanukah candles are sacred — we are permitted only to

look at, not to use them. The fulfillment of God's commandments, the objects of holiness, were not meant for man's personal gratification. One who looks at the symbols of the revelation of His sanctity does not think of his own personal gratification. Rather, he is filled with a sense of humility, with a desire to utter thanks and praise to God.

But the Sabbath lights represent *Shalom Bayit*; hence, one may make use of their light, for the gratification of body and soul. For peace was given to us to benefit our lives.

During the weekdays our souls are under a cloud. The labors our bodies endure, the burdens we carry physically, are burdens to our souls as well, darkening their light. Holiness and purity, joy and pleasure, truth and faithfulness, peace and serenity — all are soul forces and lights. During the week, these lights are covered by the clouds of the profane. But when the Sabbath comes and the body rests from its labor, the soul too regains its strength, reveals its force, and radiates its light to men. The first ray of light with which the Sabbath illuminates our souls is peace.

And, as the soul is illuminated with the light of peace, so the children of Israel kindle the light of peace in their homes. By that light their faces are lit up and they regard one another in the full radiance of love and peace.

The poorest of the poor, the richest of the rich — all are obligated to kindle the Sabbath light, the light of peace. With his last penny, the poor man purchases a Sabbath candle. The wealthy man, whose home shines brilliantly throughout the week, must kindle a candle set aside specially for the Sabbath, for the peace, with the setting of the sun on the sixth day of the week. His home may not need this light for illumination, but his heart and soul do need it — and that light is the light of *Shalom Bayit*.

It is a sacred custom in many Jewish communities for fathers to bless their sons and daughters when they arrive home from the synagogue on the eve of Sabbath. The father places his hands on the heads of his children, looks at the Sabbath lights, concentrates on thoughts of heaven, and recites the blessing: (for a son) "May God make thee like Ephraim and Menasseh, (for a daughter) may God make thee like Sarah, Rebecca, Rachel, and Leah. May the Lord bless thee and keep thee. May the Lord cause his countenance to shine upon thee, and may He grant thee grace. May the Lord lift up His countenance toward thee, and give thee peace." The children answer, Amen.

Whatever anger and resentment the members of the household

have felt toward one another during the week are banished on the Sabbath. Their hearts are filled with blessing and peace in the light of the Sabbath, the light of peace.

Then the angels of peace that accompany every Jew on the Sabbath day are welcomed: "Peace be unto ye, O ministering angels, angels of peace . . . Come ye in peace, O angels of peace . . . Bless me for peace . . . May your departure be in peace."

The sanctification of the day is then uttered over wine, the blessing of peace preceding the blessing of sanctification.

Our sages taught us: "He who has not enough money to buy these things — lights for Chanukah, wine for the sanctification of the Sabbath, and lights for the Sabbath — if he has not enough to purchase them all, then the Sabbath lights take precedence over the lights of Chanukah, and the Sabbath light takes precedence over the wine for the sanctification of the Sabbath day" (Tractate Sabbath 23). For nothing is more important than peace.

PEACE ALWAYS PREVAILS

No sacrifice is too dear for peace. The good it leaves in its wake is inestimable. Peace is so strong it can always prevail. Quarreling, strife, dissension, though they fill a home, can be routed by the determination of the head of the house to keep the peace. And that peace becomes in his hand a weapon strong enough to demolish all enmity, every enemy the angels of destruction may send against him and his.

In the end, all men will make peace with him of their own free will — that is his reward for having chosen peace.

Great is peace, for all who enter its realm depart in peace.

■ WHEN PEACE DOES NOT PREVAIL

There are times when difficulties arise which husband and wife cannot overcome and cure. In a rare instance, it transpires that the covenant of marriage cannot succeed, even after the couple had put all their efforts into preserving the peace of the home. How unfortunate are the people who find themselves in this situation. A Heavenly decree prevents them from living together in peace.

It is better for a man and woman to whom it is obvious that peace will never be their lot, that they be parted and that they should not continue to live togeher. For if there can be no peace between them, then the flames of dissension will constantly flicker, and those flames will consume them both.

Husband and wife are designed for each other before their births. Our Rabbis said: Forty days before the embryo is formed, a Heavenly voice announces: "this man's daughter is meant for that man's son." (Sotah 2) Man's search for a wife is like a search for something already his which has been lost, and when he finds her and marries her it is as if he has found what had been lost and restores it to its proper place. Originally husband and wife were one. With their marriage they return to their original unity. Thus the bond of marriage is a true and everlasting bond.

Yet nevertheless this bond can be freed by a divorce.

One might have thought that the possibility of divorce would weaken the marriage bond and throw its shadow on every dissension and quarrel between man and wife. But the opposite is true.

For the possibility of divorce in Judaism is something which strengthens the marriage bond by making it one of will and consent, and not one of compulsion.

An investigation amongst all the peoples of the earth can only testify to the pre-eminence of the Jewish people in the realm of domestic peace. Amongst traditionally conscious Jews a case of divorce occurs once amongst thousands of marriages. On the other hand, those nations who tried to improve upon what was enjoined in the Torah, by making the marriage bond eternal and indissoluble, have given rise to a great many broken and torn families; — how much blood is shed on this account and how immense is the hatred in families where marriage has proved to be unsuccessful.

The law allowing divorce is for the Jew only one amongst the many laws and commandments which God has commanded His people to observe. Concerning all of them God made His covenant with the children of Israel that they should observe them for their own good. And the children of Israel are keepers of covenants. They keep the covenant with their God and each of them keeps his covenant with his mate. These two covenants watch over each other.

It is said of the Torah and her commandments: "Her ways are ways of pleasantness and all her paths are peace." (Proverbs 3, 17.) Every departure from these ways whether by addition or subtraction is a deviation from the path of the Torah to an area where there is neither pleasantness nor peace. Anyone who seeks more mercy that he finds in the Torah will end up with cruelty; anyone who seeks more faithfulness than that required by the Torah, will end up with treachery; and anyone who seeks more peace than what is enjoined by the Torah will end up with strife. "All her paths are peace" — even those which seem to involve discord; the law of divorce is given for the peace of man and the unity of the family. Those who divorce when they must, bring good upon themselves, not evil.

But even though the Torah permits divorce, this is something to be done with fear and trembling, not arbitrarily; only where every hope of healing the breach has been lost. Every Jew shares the grief of husband and wife who are to be divorced, and every one tries to reconcile them — if that is still possible.

53

RABBINIC SAYINGS ON PEACE

Rabbi Shimeon the son of Gamliel said: The world rests on three things, on law on truth and on peace. (Aboth 1.)

Those who lived in the Holy land — when they saw which of two people engaged in a quarrel stopped first, used to say: "this one is of finer Jewish stock." (Kiddushin 71.)

A man should be kindly and not demanding in his house. (Bamidbar Rabbah 89.)

Resh Lakish said: Through anger the wise man loses his wisdom. (Pesachim 66.)

"Anger in the household is like a worm among sesame seeds" (Sotah 3) — which are so small that the good and worm-eaten ones, are indistinguishable, so that all are lost.

■ CHAPTER 7

■ A LIBERAL SPIRIT

■ However wise a person may be, however straighforward and honest, he cannot attain a liberal and expansive spirit until he lives in a proper residence. Going about his daily business, he finds life humdrum. But when he comes home, to a home that he thinks attractive and a wife he thinks lovely, his spirit expands. For there he is content.

The scholar is never content, for there is always more and more knowledge for him to learn. The business man who has one hundred dollars wants two hundred, if he has two hundred he wants four hundred. He can never achieve half of what he wants. And then people are always consumed with envy of their fellow men.

His home is the only place where a man can find contentment. It is his house, his wife, his children — they all belong together. The furnishings are theirs, and they are just right for the family. His little world is complete. At home, a person need not look elsewhere for satisfaction. His home is his *Chupah*, his wife his bride, the furnishings of home best men and bridesmaids.

CREATIVITY

God gave man three precious gifts: wisdom, understanding, and knowledge. These distinguish human beings from animals. Understanding is the product of wisdom. Knowledge is the creative force which enables us to summarize the wisdom we have gained from our teachers, and the understanding we have gotten from our wisdom, and to apply them in concrete ways.

The wisdom we learn gives us the strength to withstand the trials of life. Ask a man what the purpose is of all life's troubles, and he may answer: "I have been taught that 'man is born unto labor, as the sparks fly upward.'" Ask him how he can achieve his end in life, the road being so long. He may reply: "Experience has taught me: 'Though thy beginning was small, yet thy end should greatly increase.'"

Ask him how he can keep from failing, the taskmasters being so harsh, the conditions of life so rigorous, himself so weak.

And he will retort: "I have seen in time that those who are on high go down, and those who are below go up." This is what wisdom teaches man.

Understanding, on the other hand, is a thing men attain on their own. It opens up new horizons, new prospects. But until he has digested his wisdom and his understanding and turned them into practical knowledge, a man cannot be creative. For wisdom sometimes leaves us in error, and understanding at times deceives. Knowledge alone subjects wisdom and understanding to the test of concrete reality. When what a man builds through knowledge corresponds firmly to the wisdom and understanding that preceded his knowledge, he becomes a partner in the act of creation.

In the words of the Book of Proverbs:

> "The Lord by wisdom founded the earth; by understanding He established the heavens. By His knowledge the depths were broken up, and the skies drop down their dew."

The earth was founded by wisdom. The heavens were established by understanding. But of what value are heaven and earth without fruitfulness and procreation, continuous creativity? "The depths were broken up": overflowing rivers water the earth. "The skies drop down their dew": rain from the sky revivifies all things, all things become fruitful and increase, create and renew. How? "By His knowledge."

The same holds for man. At first he acquires strength in order to be strong. Then he acquires understanding, which enables him to understand by himself the things he has learned. When the times comes for him to build a family, he is in need of knowledge. And knowledge requires practical ability, a sense of proportion, freedom of action, and freedom from the compulsions of jealousy, shame, or fear. Only he who is happy and content with his lot, and is not dependent on others, has the capacity to build a home and family on which the divine blessing may rest. The expansiveness of spirit he requires to build a home is in turn enhanced by a home where there is *Shalom Bayit.*

A FINE HOME

"Said Rabbah the son of Chanah in the name of Rabbi Yochanan, quoting Rabbi Judah the son of Elai: 'Eat less and drink less, and add the savings to the maintenance of your dwelling'" (Pesahim 114). It depresses a man to eat and drink well when he cannot afford it; but a fine home is a gratification.

"A man rejoices when he lives in a home he owns" (Jerusalem Talmud Nedarim, ch. 2). A man's spirit expands when he lives in a home he owns, though it be less elegant than a rented home.

It is a wise thing to save all one can to buy a home of one's own.

Hospitality and charity dignify a home. A home achieves importance through serving as a meeting place for scholars and community leaders.

BEAUTY IN WOMEN

"Who is rich? Rabbi Akiba said: 'He who has a wife whose ways are pleasant'" (Tractate Sabbath 25 b).

Rabbi Akiba's wife Rachel helped him acquire wisdom. Her father was wealthy, but she gave up all the comforts of her father's home to follow her husband. They lived in poverty for many years in a tumbledown hut, sleeping on straw. Rabbi Akiba pursued the study of the Torah while Rachel helped and encouraged him. When they grew old they became wealthy and "both Torah and material comfort dwelt at their table."

But all the years of his material poverty Rabbi Akiba was never downcast, for the Lord had blessed him with wealth — in the form of his wife, Rachel. All the years Rabbi Akiba lived in poverty with Rachel, whose ways were truly beautiful, he felt himself the richest man in the world.

A woman of valour who can find?
For her price is far above rubies.
The heart of her husband doth safely trust in her .
And he hath no lack of gain.
She doeth him good and not evil
All the days of her life.
She seeketh wool and flax
And worketh willingly with her hands.
She is like the merchant-ships
She bringeth her food from afar.
She riseth also while it is yet night
And giveth food to her household
And a portion to her maidens.
She considereth a field and buyeth it
With the fruit of her hands she planteth a vineyard.
She girdeth her loins with strength,
And maketh strong her arms.
She perceiveth that her merchandise is good.
Her lamps goeth not out by night.
She layeth her hands to the distaff
And her hands hold the spindle.
She stretches out her hand to the poor.
Yea, she reacheth forth her hands to the needy.
She is not afraid of the snow for her household;
For all her household are clothed with scarlet.
She maketh for herself coverlets
Her clothing is fine linen and purple.
Her husband is known in the gates,
When he sitteth among the elders of the land.
She maketh linen garments and selleth them
And delivereth girdles unto the merchant.
Strength and dignity are her clothing;
And she laugheth at a latter day.
She openeth her mouth with wisdom;
And the law of kindness is on her tongue.
She looketh well to the ways of her household,
and eateth not the bread of idleness.
Her children rise up and call her blessed;
Her husband also, and he praiseth her:
"Many daughters have done valiantly,
But thou excelleth them all."
Grace is deceitful, and beauty is vain;
But a woman that feareth the Lord, she shall be praised.
Give her of the fruit of her hands;
And let her works praise her in the gates.

(Proverbs **XXXI**, 10-31)

CHAPTER 8

■ A WOMAN OF VALOR

■ "A woman of valor who can find; for her price is far above rubies."

A Jewish sage said: This psalm is in praise of the woman who deliberately gives up her father's ways in favor of those of her husband, to whom she becomes as a sister; who smiles upon him even when he is angry; who honors him in poverty as well as in wealth, in old age as in youth. She is slow to leave home but quick to give bread to the poor. Though she have many servants, she does not sit idly by, but works with them. She is attentive to those who address her, but not hasty in response. She is happy with her husband's happiness, and a source of hope to him when he is burdened with woe. Her ways are seemly, and she is clad in modesty.

WOMEN AS AGENTS OF REDEMPTION

Jewish tradition relates that it was the righteous women who enabled our forefathers to be redeemed and brought forth out of Egypt. The husbands had grown apathetic and abandoned hope. "What," the men said to themselves, "are we to bring children into the world to be slaves and suffer like us?" They refused to have intercourse with their wives. But the women, though sharing their husbands' slavery and suffering, encouraged them to hope. They deliberately sought out their husbands' love. It was they who were responsible for the birth of a new generation, fit to be redeemed.

For the women reasoned: "True, the children we bear now will be at the mercy of our enemies, yet let us bear them. For in time to come He who watches us from on high will save our children and deliver them out of the land of Egypt."

This has been true for the Jewish people in other lands than Egypt. In every generation, at the very hour when all seemed hopeless, virtuous Jewish women have sweetened their husbands' lives, consoled them in times of adversity, and kindled the spark of hope for better times.

WEALTH AND HONOR

It is written: "He whom God has blessed with a good wife will never lack, though he be poor in material goods. For Scripture states: 'The heart of her husband doth safely trust in her, and he hath no lack of gain.' And it is further written: 'A woman of valor who can find; for her price is far above rubies.'"

"Happy is he and happy his lot who was merited a good wife. For through her he will win the respect of others; as Scripture says: 'A virtuous wife is a crown to her husband.'"

CHILDLESSNESS

The hardest thing for husband and wife to bear is childlessness. Though they have everything else, without children they feel themselves deprived. The thing they long for most is healthy children. Yet, though children be denied them by nature, they can acquire children through divine blessing — through the wife's love.

Our sages relate:

"In Sidon there was a man and wife who lived together for ten years without producing children. They came to Rabbi Simon the son of Yochai for a separation.

"Said he to them: 'By your lives, as you were wedded with food and drink, so you shall be parted.'

"They obeyed him, and prepared a banquet. During the feast, the wife made the husband drunk.

"He said to her: 'My daughter, choose whatever object you think most precious in our home and take it with you back to your father's home.'

"When her husband fell asleep, the wife called her servants and said, 'Carry him to my father's house.' Late at night he awoke.

" 'My daughter,' he said, 'where am I?'

" 'In my father's house,' she replied.

" 'What am I doing in your father's house?'

" 'Didn't you tell me this evening to choose the object I consider most precious and take it with me to my father's house? You are the most precious thing in the world to me!'

"They returned to Rabbi Simon the son of Yochai. Rabbi Simon rose and prayed in their behalf, and they were blessed with offspring." (Song of Songs, Midrash Rabba 1)

Had Rabbi Simon prayed for them when they first came to him, it is doubtful that his request would have been granted. But afterward, it was certain to be granted. For Rabbi Simon was able to come to God with a just argument:

"Thou hast fashioned Thy world with benevolence and love. See how greatly this woman loves her husband, how without any ulterior motive! Shall He who loves all of His creatures not show mercy to these two? Master of the universe, if Thou dost not grant children to these two loving companions, Thou shalt be causing a separation between two who cleave to each other. But if Thou grant them children as a remembrance, their love will be forever!"

HUSBAND'S RIGHTEOUSNESS

"Once a pious man was married to a pious woman, but they had no children. Said they: 'We are unproductive to God,' and were divorced. Later the husband married an evil woman, and she turned him toward evil. The wife married an evil man, and she turned him toward good. From which we see how everything proceeds from the woman."

ORIGIN OF GOOD

Would you know the role the wife's piety plays in our tradition, study the Torah.

The first man to be called the father of all his generations until the end of time was Abraham, who was called, "the father of a multitude of nations." Isaac and Jacob, too, were called the fathers of all the generations to come.

Eve was the first to be called "the mother of all living," anticipating, in this, the wives of Abraham, Isaac, and Jacob. Adam was never called "the father of all living," being known simply as "the first man." Proving that motherhood is an earlier, deeper, and more lasting mark than fatherhood.

In nature, respect for motherhood takes precedence over respect for fatherhood. That is why the Torah found it necessary to put "father" first in the commandment: "Honor thy father and thy mother" — that both might be respected equally. Since nature gives precedence to the mother, the Torah redresses the balance by mentioning the father first.

Abraham was unique. He saved himself and the whole world from paganism, and brought the world back to God. God revealed Himself to Abraham, and he became a prophet of God for his own and succeeding generations. A mortal can aspire to no higher excellence than that conferred by prophecy, by the capacity to hear the word of God. And yet, high as was Abraham's excellence, Sarah's was higher still. For the Lord said to Abraham: "In all that Sarah saith unto thee, hearken unto her voice." The fact is that after Sarah's death, the blessing that her virtue conferred on her house ceased, only to be restored by the appearance of Rebecca.

"So long as Sarah was alive, the cloud of God's presence hung over the entrance to her home. When she died, the cloud passed. It returned when Rebecca entered that house. So long as Sarah was alive, the doors of her home were open wide in hospitality; when Sarah died, the doors were closed. On Rebecca's arrival, they opened wide again. So long as Sarah was alive, the bread was blessed, as a sign that she had not wasted her husband's substance. When Sarah died that blessing ceased, to return only with the appearance of Rebecca. So long as Sarah was alive, a light burned in the home from Sabbath eve to Sabbath eve, as a sign of Shalom Bayit. On her death the light was extinguished. When Rebecca came the light began to burn again from Sabbath eve to Sabbath eve."

Until the birth of our savior in Egypt, Moses, our forefathers had lost the hope of being redeemed. Even Amram, Moses's father, who was the leader of his generation, seeing no hope, separated from his wife Yocheved, so as not to bring children into a world of slavery. Following Amram's example, other men did the same. Then his daughter came to Amram and said to him:

"You are acting more cruelly than Pharaoh. For Pharaoh has decreed that all male children born to the Hebrews are to be cast into the river; you are decreeing against female children, as well!"

Hearing this, Amram had a change of heart. He returned to Yocheved, who bore him Moses, the savior of Israel. The other Hebrews in Egypt returned to their wives. They were fruitful and multiplied, bringing a new generation into the world, one that was to be redeemed. His sister Miriam saved Moses again, when his life was in danger and he had been cast into the river. It was Miriam who was responsible for the first step in the salvation of the Hebrews in Egypt and of all Israel to come.

When Israel committed the sin of worshipping the golden calf in the wilderness, the women resisted. Their husbands forced them against their will to remove their jewels and give them up for the decoration of the golden calf. For the women were always more loyal to God than were the men. When the men who had been sent out to spy on the land of Canaan returned with their reports of fortified cities that were impregnable, causing consternation among the Hebrews in the desert, and the cry: "Let us return to Egypt" — the women were not frightened. The men rejected the Promised Land: "They scorned the desirable land." But, according to Jewish tradition, the women continued to love the land. Scripture relates how intensely the daughters of Zelophead were concerned over their inheritance in the land of Canaan. God's decree punishing the children of Israel for blaspheming the land: "In this wilderness they shall be consumed, and there they shall die" applied to the men only, not to the women.

During the period of the judges, there was no king in Israel and each man did what was proper in his eyes. The entire nation did the evil in the eyes of the Lord, serving false gods. Then the anger of the Lord was kindled against them and He gave them over into the hands of their foes. "Now Deborah, a prophetess, the wife of Lappidoth, she judged Israel at that time." Deborah arose, a mother in Israel, to help heal the wounds of the people.

Later, there was a famine in the land, and the hearts of the men of Judah were full of fear. When their leaders left the land to sojourn in the fields of Moab, the rest of the people became despondent, saying: "If Elimelech and his sons have left because of the famine, how shall we survive?"

God would not forgive Elimelech and his children this desertion of the land, and struck them dead in the land of Moab. But He did not strike down Naomi, the wife of Elimelech, because she did not share her husband's guilt. All the years of her stay in the foreign land she had refused to be comforted for having left the Promised Land — though Moab was prosperous and flourishing. Impatiently, Naomi awaited the day when God would remember His people with bread in their own land, and she might return thither. And when she returned to the land of Judah, she brought with her a treasure more precious than gems, her daughter-in-law, Ruth the Moabite.

Ruth came of an ungrateful stock — the people of Moab, of whom Scripture declares: "They shall not enter the assembly of the Lord ... for ever, because they met you not with bread and with water in the way when ye came forth out of Egypt" — though themselves descended from Abraham's nephew Lot, who would have been killed by the Five Kings were it not for Abraham. But Ruth, despite her ancestry, was kind, compassionate, loving, and appreciative. Her husband Nahlon and father-in-law Elimelech were of Hebrew stock, of the tribe of Judah, whose very name signifies "thanksgiving." Eventually, Israel's royal family was to descend from the tribe of Judah. Yet, in time of famine, the men of Judah had deserted the land of their people. It was a foreign woman, Ruth, the Moabite, who was to be the ancestress of the royal family of Israel, the kingdom of the house of David, destined to last forever.

When the wicked Haman sought to destroy all the Jews in the land of Persia, Esther and Mordecai saved their people. Esther did not covet the "half of the kingdom" which the king of Persia offered her. Rather she asked: "Let my life be given me at my petition, and my people at my request." The Jews of Persia had "a sister in the palace of the king." Esther's eyes were directed to heaven: "And if I perish, I perish." She had perished in the palace once, she thought, and she was prepared to perish again seeking to save her people.

"What merit did Esther possess that she reigned over 'a hundred and seven and twenty provinces'?"

"God said: 'May the daughter of Sarah, who lived for a hundred and seven and twenty years, reign over a hundred and seven and twenty provinces.'" (Midrash Esther 1). For, indeed, Esther was a true daughter of Sarah. Esther was like Sarah in beauty, in modesty, and in purity even when queen of the Persians. Sarah was the ancestress of the people whom Esther saved from destruction.

In the days of Mattathias the son of the high priest Jochanan, the kingdom of Syria tried to force the Jews to abandon the Torah and to forsake God's laws. But it was not Mattathias and his sons who were the first to signal revolt — it was his daughter. She and her friends challenged the people of the Lord to rebel.

The Syrians had prohibited the observance of the Sabbath and the covenant of circumcision. Headed by Mattathias's daughter, the daughters of Israel appeared on the city walls, their infants in their arms. And there, in the view of all, they circumcised the children — then flung themselves off the wall to die with their children.

With this act of martyrdom, they were saying to their husbands and brothers: "If you will not go forth to fight the enemy, you will have neither wives nor children!" The men went forth to battle, and were victorious.

Judith was still another heroine who bravely avenged her people. Returning to the Jewish camp with the head of Holofernes, the Syrian general, she infused new courage in her brothers' hearts. Earlier, during the Hasmonean revolt, when the land lay under the heels of the Syrian tyrant, another woman, Hannah, taught the people of Israel how to sanctify the name of God in death.

And when times of sorrow came, and the land of Israel was conquered by oppressors who defiled the sanctuary of God and attempted to eradicate Judaism from the Jewish people, it was Hannah, the mother of seven sons, who was the first to teach the nation the lesson of martyrdom.

And in every generation, in times of oppression as in times of relief, in the latest generations just as in the earliest, every good trait one finds in our people and amongst its leaders, is the result of the influence of a Jewish mother — more than a Jewish father. To such an extent is this apparent that it has become a proverbial truth: "Show me a great man and I will show you a great mother."

It is therefore plain that the origin of everything good that one finds in the world and amongst Jews is woman. Eve was the mother of all living creatures; Sarah, the mother of prophecy; Miriam, the mother of salvation; The women of the generation of the exodus were the mothers of pure faith; Deborah was the mother of heroism; Ruth, the mother of royalty; Esther, the mother of redemption; Judith, the daughter of Mattathias, and the women of her generation, were the mothers of rebellion; Hannah with her seven sons, the mother of martyrdom. And the righteous and pious Jewish women of our generation are the mothers of the Messianic era.

65

THE CROWN OF MODESTY

We have enumerated many of the superior advantages that women have over men. Why then do men consider themselves superior? And why are the religious duties of man more extensive than those of women? Why does a man thank God every morning "that Thou hast not made me a woman"?

The one answer to these three questions lies in a characteristic which women have and men have not — something special which dominates all their other qualities.

Two people equal in talents and rank are offered promotion. One accepts it while the other does not. The latter may refuse because of modesty. He feels satisfied with the position which he occupies and has no wish to "ascend higher." He is thereby morally superior to his friend, for he has shown himself to be more modest, and nothing ranks higher than modesty.

When a wife allows her husband to lead the family she demonstrates her moral superiority, and this is the respect in which she takes precedence over him. Of all the wonderful qualities possessed by woman, modesty is the most exalted.

Every law and ordinance, every warning and punishment, and all the commandments that were given by God to His creatures, were given to them for their own benefit, so that man may live by them. They are thus to be regarded as privileges. Would the Creator of the world in lovingkindness and mercy have discriminated between creature and creature and given more privileges to one than to another? Man and woman are of the same species, and their understanding and intelligence are equal — is it then possible that there should not be the same Torah for both? No, indeed it is not. And Scripture expressly regards men and women as equal in respect of all the commandments of the Torah.

Nevertheless there are commandments in the Torah from which women are exempted, namely, the majority of positive command-ments the performance of which is restricted to a set time, such as Tzitzith (fringes) and Tephillin (phylacteries) which must be worn in the day only; Shofar, Succah (Tabernacles), Lulab, etc., which are restricted to certain days of the Jewish year.

But the exemption of women from the performance of these commandments has nothing to do with any alleged inferiority. On the contrary, it is a sign of their superiority.

For not only women are exempt from certain commandments in the Torah. It sometimes happens that men too are exempted from some commandments. For example if a man is already engaged in the performance of a commandment and a second commandment presents itself, then he is exempt from performing the second commandment. In some cases commandments become obligatory which involve the overriding of other commandments. A classical example of this in the Talmud is the case of a Nazir (see Numbers VI, 2, a man who is, amongst other things, forbidden to come into contact with dead human bodies), who is at the same time a High Priest (for whom such contact is still more stringently forbidden) — about to slaughter the Passover-offering and to circumcise his son (two commandments the transgression of which involves the most severe of penalties). If he learns of the death of one of his nearest relatives, he is not allowed to attend to the actual burial, since his status forbids him to come into contact with dead bodies. But if he finds an unburied corpse for whom there is no one else to care, he is not only permitted but duty-bound to violate his status as a Nazir and as a priest, to disregard the Passover-offering and the circumcision of his son, to disregard every other commandment and to perform this one commandment. His exemption from all other commandments is certainly no sign of inferiority; he is exempt from them because a more important duty rests upon him at that moment.

Similarly, a scholar who devotes his life to the study of Torah, which he studies in purity and holiness, is exempt from all commandments because of the Torah which he studies. Such a man is certainly superior morally to all others and this is reflected in his being exempted from commandments.

From this it can readily be understood that if two persons are equally duty-bound to observe commandments, and one of them is exempted from some, this exemption is due to another duty which rests upon him and which does not rest upon his friend. And the exemption proves that he has more important tasks to do which cannot be done except by him.

Thus, woman, basically equal to man with regard to all the commandments of the Torah, but exempt from some which have time-limits, is proved thereby to be superior, for the special tasks which are hers, must be the reason for her exemption.

THE HIGHEST CROWN

There is no greater token of praise and appreciation of womanhood than that contained in the two blessings composed by our

Rabbis and designed to be said by men and women respectively as part of their daily prayers. A woman says: "Blessed art Thou, o Lord our God, King of the Universe who hast made me according to Thy will" (or in some versions "according to my own will"). A man says: "Blessed . . . . who hast not made me a woman."

If a man's job were given to a woman she could manage it, even if it were a little difficult for her sometimes. In fact in the modern world we do find many women doing jobs formerly performed only by men; and women succeed at these jobs very well. But if a woman's chores were imposed on a man, he could not manage them. The tasks of a woman are far more difficult than the tasks of a man, and a woman's versatility and her power of endurance are greater than a man's.

Since the hour of creation, mankind has had nothing it could really call its own except toil and labor. All other powers and talents are gifts of Providence. Man's toil, labor and burden are his contribution towards the maintenance of the world, and through them man becomes a partner in the work of creation. If a man takes from what the world has to offer and enjoys it, and gives to the world what is specifically his, then he is a partner in the work of creation and is entitled to take what he does take. But if a man takes from what the world has to offer and gives nothing to the world, and also does not bless the Creator — then he is a thief and is not entitled to what he takes. Thus a person's worth is measured by the relationship between the benefit he has from the world and the toil, labour and sweat of his brow which he gives to the world in exchange for this benefit. Now, a woman takes far less from the world than a man and in exchange she gives so much more toil, labor and effort.

Man could not be satisfied with a woman's share in life. Nor, on the other hand, could he do a woman's job, even if he tried. His share in life is easier and more pleasant. He is not able to return to the world as much as he has enjoyed. Let him at least be grateful and thank the Lord for his portion. He therefore thanks the Creator for having given him the easier lot. A man's blessing is a token of thankfulness for benefits enjoyed. And every one who benefits from the world and does not bless the Lord is called a thief.

But a woman's virtue lies in her accepting and being contented with her lot. She does not complain but blesses the Lord who has made her according to His will (or according to her own). She does not toil for the sake of a reward, but in order to fulfil the will of her Creator. Her blessing, unlike a man's, is not a blessing in exchange for benefits, but a blessing in exchange for toil. And she testifies thereby that her toil is dearer to her than any benefit.

This may be illustrated by the following parable:

A king orders his army out to war. No man can say "I do not want to go to war" or, "I want to go home from the front"; this would be desertion.

When a man returns home after the war the king rewards him. But no man can say I do not want any reward and I don't want to fight. If he says so he is a traitor — everyone must go to war when the king commands.

There are times when a king asks for volunteers for a particularly difficult and dangerous task. The volunteers come forward and risk their lives to accomplish the task; the others watch them from afar with awe and fear. Those who did not volunteer bless the king for not having assigned the difficult task to them, which they would never have been able to perform. And the volunteers bless the king and thank him for having been chosen to do the task, in accordance with his will, and their will.

The desire to achieve greatness is one of the most human of characteristics, and many who do not succeed in obtaining the recognition which they think they deserve become embittered and broken in spirit. Few and rare are those individuals who do not care for greatness and are content to live modestly and happily; who may be engaged in works which benefit the whole of mankind, but avoid publicity and prefer to let others bask in undeserved glory.

This trait is woman's glory. Modesty is the dominant virtue in her character. She is the initiator, the founder, the source of so much that is good. Yet she herself stands modestly in the shadow and lets others bask in honor and glory.

She is the "mother of all life" in her essence, and "helpmate" in her appearance. She is the mother of pure faith, of dedication to good and war against iniquity, yet she appears to the world as the dedicated wife who lets her husband take all the credit.

Adam, Seth, Enosh, Noah, Shem and Eber, Abraham, Isaac and Jacob, Moses and Aaron, Joshua, the Judges, Prophets, Kings — and the Messiah himself — these are the "revealed" part of God's plan with the world. Eve and Naama (Noah's wife), Sarah, Rebecca, Rachel and Leah, Jochebed and Miriam, Deborah and Jael, Naomi and Ruth and all the righteous and saintly women through all the generations, every wife faithful to her husband and mother devoted to her children — these are the hidden and "secret" part of God's plan for the universe. No status could be more exalted than hers.

EQUAL RIGHTS

In view of what has been said, it is easy to understand why our Rabbis did not engage in empty talk about "woman's equal rights" or "the restoration of woman's honor." The Jewish People, living as it does, according to God's laws and His Torah, never denied woman her rights and would not be able, even if they wanted, to give woman more rights than she possesses. Man and woman are king and queen — each rules in a different world. Each has different tasks and different sorts of rights. They hold two stations of equal rank but one kingdom has no connection at all with the other. Man is the revealed part of the world, woman its secret part. Man conquers and woman gives him the strength to do so. Man is the trunk of the tree, woman the hidden well from which the tree draws its sustenance. Man's activities are broad, all-embracing and visible — and this is his advantage over woman. But woman's activities are of more lasting value and her influence is more permanent — and this is her advantage over man.

The sons and daughters of a Jewish woman, even if she is married to a non-Jew, are regarded as Jewish children. And even if her daughters should marry non-Jews their offspring will be Jewish. And so on for ever. But in the case of a Jewish man who marries a non-Jewess, their children are non-Jewish. For the influence of a mother lasts on her children forever, but the influence of the father is so short-lived that it may be wiped out immediately. And the Holy One Blessed be He, found no vessel more suited to motherhood and to act as a source of everlasting influence, than modesty. That is why he implanted modesty in womankind.

Indeed, the rights of a woman in her husband's home are defined by the Rabbis as follows:

"She goes up with him but does not go down with him. Rabbi Elazar said: We learn this from the verse 'Because she was the mother of all that lives' (Gen. III, 20) — she was given to her husband to live and not to suffer." (Kethuboth 61.)

Thus a woman marries a husband to improve her lot and not vice-versa. If she was hitherto accustomed to a higher standard of living than her husband then he must maintain her in that high standard. But if she was hitherto accustomed to a lower standard of living than her husband, then he must provide for her according to his higher standard.

RABBINIC SAYINGS ON THE GOOD WIFE

"But he that is of merry heart hath a continual feast" (Proverbs 15:15) — this refers to the man who has a good wife (Baba Bathra 145).

"Jewish girls are not noisy nor continually running around, nor given to light-headed laughter" (Tanchumah).

"A woman does not sit idle" (Yerushalmi, Kethuboth 82).

It is written in the book of Ben-Sira: "A good wife is a precious gift given to him who fears the Lord; a bad wife is a plague to her husband. Happy is the husband of a beautiful wife — his number of days are doubled."

"A bashful woman is charming, and a restrained soul is priceless" (Ben-Sira).

"A woman who honors her husband appears wise to all" (Ibid).

"A noisy and sharp-tongued woman is as frightening as a trumpet of war" (Ibid).

"Any ache but heartache, and any evil but that of an evil wife" (Shabbath II).

CHAPTER 9

■ MODESTY AND CONDUCT

■ Modesty has an enduring value, one that is unsurpassed for the pleasure and peace of mind it affords. It should be the concern of everyone, whether he be man or woman, adult or child. It covers the whole wide range of all life's relationships, at home and in the family as well as abroad.

MODESTY AT HOME

It is the better part of wisdom for the head of the household to introduce the discipline of modesty at home at the very beginning of family life.

He must not permit his home to seethe with noise, screaming, loud laughter, bitter cries of anger.

Pleasure-seekers will not be welcome in his home; though he be a man of means, he will avoid conspicuous consumption or ostentation.

His table will not be richly laden at ordinary meals. The members of his household will not overeat, or drink to the point of intoxication. They will not be pleasure-seeking butterflies.

They will not rise at noon and go to sleep at midnight. It will be early to bed and early to rise for them.

On the other hand, he must avoid the other extreme — ascetic self-denial. Moderation must be the key word.

The yard stick should be this: Eschew as immodest any pattern of behavior so out of keeping with one's life situation that it would elicit the amazed comment of outsiders.

It is foolish to envy those for whom life is one big party, one round of celebrations. They are no index to real happiness. For we often fail to see the suffering and torment in the hearts of those who feel they must be always dancing.

There is a time for everything: If you see a person resting when he should be resting, and calm when tranquillity is called for, you can be sure that he is really happy when he dances on some special occasion.

Modesty, means proper moderation, in food and drink, in hospitality, speech, in relations within the family and outside it. A visitor will immediately breathe the air of sweet calm and peace. He will enjoy his stay and leave with the prayer that this home may remain thus serene forever.

SPEECH

Soft speech is the best safeguard of a home's serenity. Watch carefully the shopkeeper behind the counter, the laborer at work, the teacher in the classroom — who is the more effective? The man who is always shouting and yelling? Or the one whose manner is restrained, who speaks in a low voice? The latter is always more sympathetic, consequently more persuasive.

The same is true of the home and family, where so much that is of abiding significance takes place. In forging unity of hearts, in rearing children and educating them, nothing is worse than tumult. God is not to be found in the tempest — those who walk in His ways should emulate the Lord, speaking humbly, in subdued and quiet voices.

A quiet house is a tranquil house. Everyone is heard, no one is overpowered. Words go from mouth to ear, from ear to heart. And the habit of soft speech is easy to achieve, requiring only moderate effort. Newly-weds who practice restraint in speech from the very beginning are on their way to turning their home into a haven of serenity and a fortress of security.

MODESTY BETWEEN HUSBAND AND WIFE

The sages said: "A groom may not go under the wedding canopy without the bride's consent."

This saying, properly applied, can be a guidepost for every aspect of the relations between husband and wife. Both are to abstain even from actions which are permitted, if viewed as immodest or if both do not agree on it.

"Said Rav Chisda to his daughters: 'Be modest in the presence of your husband. Do not eat in excess or coarsely in the presence of your husbands. Do not eat strong-smelling vegetables at night; abstain from dates and strong drink at night (whose effects are purgative).'"

IN THE SIGHT OF OUTSIDERS

We have noted above that a poor style of life for a person of average or above-average means is as immodest as an extravagant style. Similarly, a disorderly, dirty, messy home is a sign of immodesty, evokes the disdain of outsiders, and, ultimately, self-depreciation.

Modesty is desirable in all things, all relations, all actions, within the family, at home, and with outsiders. We have mentioned speech, food, furniture, cleanliness, relations between husband and wife, parents and children, the family as a whole and outsiders. Let us begin with clothing.

CLOTHING

Clothing is a mark of man's uniqueness. Of all the many creatures God created, none but man was given clothing. And it was God Himself who first clothed man: "And the Lord God made for Adam and for his wife garments of skins and clothed them."

Of course, Adam and Eve were not clothed until after they had committed the transgression of eating of the fruit of the Tree of Knowledge. Before that "they were both naked, the man and his wife, and were not ashamed." It was only after he had sinned that Adam said: "I was afraid, because I was naked; and I hid myself." Still, God had intended to grant man the gift of clothing from the beginning. But Adam did not merit this gift until he felt shame at his wrongdoings. True, Adam sinned. But his regret and contrition protected him from loss of honor and degradation.

With divine lovingkindness God overlooked Adam's sin. The Holy One, blessed be He, said to Adam: "Since you are ashamed of the wrong you have committed, and your nakedness makes you afraid, I will give you garments to cover your nakedness, and with it, your transgression." That is the true meaning of the verse in Scripture: "He made them garments of skins and clothed them."

Hence, when dressed properly, a man is honored; when not dressed properly, or undressed, he is dishonored. He is like a person caught in a shameful act who displays his shame without embarrassment, thinking: "Having been caught and disgraced once, I may as well do it again."

MAN'S SUPERIORITY TO THE BEAST

Man is the only living creature capable of both merit and error. The other creatures were assigned by God to specific tasks. They were given unchangeable natures. This being so, there is no room for merit or error — they but perform the tasks assigned them by nature. Hence, they can have no sense of shame. They are never embarrassed by anything they do; their actions are all transparent.

Man's task is far loftier than that of any beast, and as a consequence he is capable of both merit and error; for he is not bound by nature to fulfill an appointed task. He can do so if he so desires; if he does not, he deviates from his human task. The fulfillment of the divinely assigned task we call merit; the deviation from it, error. Hence, too, man knows shame, insofar as he becomes aware of the damage his misdeeds inflict on God's creation and on himself.

None of the other creatures know the taste of sin. But sin is a constant companion of man. And yet, nevertheless, he remains superior to all the other creatures. Why? Because only he is meritorious who, having the capacity to do wrong, does not. Even if he should succumb to temptation, the shame that follows sinning raises man again to his proper estate. The very punishment that is divinely inflicted on man, whether he be aware of it or not, saves him from ultimate degradation by redressing the balance of his life. As a result, we find that in the final accounting, the lives of both the good man and the wicked balance out. The righteousness of the good man balances out his sins, the suffering of the wicked balances his. Good or bad, man's superiority to the rest of creation remains great. As we have noted, man merited the divine gift of clothing, which no other creature received, because of his innate excellence.

DISTINCTIONS AMONG MEN

As men as a whole are distinguished from beasts, so there are degrees of distinction among men. One man's transgression is never the same as another's; their subsequent sense of shame are naturally dissimilar; clothing that may be proper for one person may be improper for another.

God has placed merit and error in balanced contrast. The more virtuous a man the greater his potential for error. For this reason, our wise sages, students of psychology, made no attempt to deny the depths of sin lurking in each man's personality, however righteous he may be. They did not try to disguise the existence of the inclination to evil (*Yetzer Hara*). Rather, they sought ways of sweetening its bitterness, restraints and curbs to hedge it about.

But our sages were keenly aware that these restraints and curbs had to be blended and measured in accordance with the differing qualities and needs of men, in accordance with the endless variety of the degrees of excellence and error to be found in human beings.

Sensual lust is at the root of many human failings and transgressions. The man who is embarrassed by his sins is inevitably embarrassed by the source of transgression. Leading him on to wrong doing, it is a constant and embarrassing reminder of his transgression. Hence, men cover the source of their failings with clothing, thus distracting themselves in thought from their sensual drives. The clothing with which men cover their physical selves reduce their sensual drives, saving them from both sin and subsequent shame.

How much of his body should a man conceal to be protected from wrong-doing and shame?

In this matter, as in many others, people are not all alike. A person's mode of dress depends on the degree of his personal excellence and on the contrasting strength of the temptations paralleling his virtue. For, as the rabbis said: "The greater the man, the stronger his *Yetzer Hara*." That is to say, he who is assigned more exalted tasks in the world than his fellow man, also possesses deeper roots of potential sin. So he needs greater protection than does he who has been assigned lesser tasks.

Man is superior to all other creatures. His superiority resides in the fact that he is subject, with all his heart and soul, to very many commandments and prohibitions which can serve him either as a source for merit or an obstacle. Hence he alone knows shame. He alone needs clothing to cover his nakedness, as a hedge against the intrusion of sin, as a protection of his glorious superiority from degradation — all things which the rest of creation has no need of.

Woman's honor is greater still than man's. For she is by nature destined to bear the burden of the world's very existence and continuation. Woman is so fashioned that perfect faithfulness of heart, love and compassion should well up from her. She can be a source of goodness for all that surround her. She can give her husband life, grace, and lovingkindness. She can fill her home with beauty and splendor.

Yet here, too, we find balance and contrast. For the dangers facing woman are as great as is her capacity for excellence. If untrue to her lofty calling, she can become the source of the lowest abomination.

Woman can choose two utterly opposite extremes — the height of glory or the depth of shame. This is her pride. Women, therefore, have a stronger sense of shame than men. Hence, too, women must guard their modesty with clothing even more carefully than men.

Clothing that might be considered modest for a man is not sufficiently modest for a woman. By modesty of attire women save both themselves and others from wrong-doing; they preserve the glory with which the Creator has crowned womankind.

The married woman is superior to the unmarried one, in that in her every potential gift of femininity becomes actual. She has entered on the fulfillment of her divinely ordained mission. She builds the home she was destined to build, filling it with everything good and blessed. She conceives and bears children, nurses, and rears them — thus building a new generation, daily renewing the act of creation. If she endures in her task, she gives her husband the strength to endure in his.

Her excellence being superior to that of the unmarried woman, the married woman must be even more on guard than her sister. She must be careful not to transgress herself or lead others astray, so that neither in thought, speech or deed may she lapse or cause others to lapse. Hence, a married woman should be more modest in dress than her unmarried sister.

What is the particular mark of the married woman's modesty?

She covers not only her body, but the hair of her head as well. A woman's hair is lovely. Reserved for her husband's eyes, her loveliness is sacred, in keeping with the laws of modesty. But,

77

exposed to the sight of others, her loveliness can be the source of profanity. Restraint, as expressed in the covering of a married woman's hair, is another means by which a woman hedges her sacredness about. Vigilance is the price of the married woman's honor.

CHAPTER 10

■ ESTEEM

■ Husband and wife are bidden to hold each other in esteem — paradoxically, *despite* their love for one another. For those who love one another often disregard what they consider the conventional trivia of courtesy.

It is a mistake for husband or wife to imagine that their mutual love and affection requires no external manifestations of simple courtesy. The truth is that esteem is the higher manifestation.

LOVE CAN DISTORT

At times love, as well as hate, can lead to some distortion of behavior. For intense emotion can lead one to cross the established bounds of conduct, to indulge in actions or words one would otherwise consider unbefitting. An appreciation of the true value of esteem, and a life lived in consonance with that appreciation, rarely results in actions that are beyond the pale and which one later regrets or is ashamed of.

People who live for the moment alone know no greater pleasure than the pleasure of the moment. They expend all their energies on that momentary pleasure. They drink past the point of enjoyment, to revulsion. At the very moment of satiety, their souls are empty. One sees them on every hand, wasting their lives in empty, unfulfilling clamor. If ever you see a husband and wife who are deeply in love but who consider themselves above the obligations of mutual respect, mocking the customary rules of courtesy, be concerned for their future. Valuing flirtation above courtesy, they end by suffering the pangs of disillusionment. For what they think is perfect love may really be no more than self-love and the outburst of the sensual instinct. Too often, such love without courtesy produces impatience and tension and the eventual breakdown of harmonious relations. For once the force of youth is spent and sensual desires abate, and forbearance becomes the test of love, the fancied love of their youth vanishes.

SELF-LOVE

Complete "freedom of behavior" between husband and wife is the result, as we have said, not of love but of self-love; and he who is entirely involved in self-love is incapable of loving another. In time, a person dominated by self-love grows impatient when the needs of others "intrude" on his own. He becomes resentful when the fulfillment of their needs imposes some inconvenience or requires some effort on his part which is not rewarded with pleasure. He reacts with anger. If he should have to make such special and frequent efforts, he grows chronically impatient; the slightest provocation causes him to explode in a paroxysm of rage. In sum: The very explosiveness of his youthful love, whose lack of restraint was but the expression of hidden selfishness, inevitably was transformed into the explosiveness of violent quarrelling and bitter hatred.

Family life cannot continuously be a matter of "sweetness and light." Every one has his troubled moments — some caused by himself, others by his wife and children. One who has not been spoiled by continual pampering, can overcome the effects of those difficult moments — and even sometimes remain capable of seeing the possible good that might follow. But he who has been pampered will rebel against every effort to "limit his freedom" — and with it, his pleasure.

THE WISE MAN SEES THE FUTURE

There are two kinds of future. One is the future that only

prophecy can reveal. A second kind is one predetermined by natural law. The understanding of either of these futures is not the province of wisdom. The only future that falls into that province is the future which it is given all men to know. But while the fool may know that future, he will never see it. Only the wise man will see it, in advance, as though it were already present.

No one is so foolish as not to know that the surging power of his youth will be followed by the level plains of middle age — these, in turn, to be followed by the downhill slope of old age. And yet, though everyone knows that, one has to be very wise to be able to see those future days, wise to be able to prepare for them in advance.

When a person enters the covenant of marriage, the years of his youth for the most part lie behind him. Most of his married life will be years of middle and old age.

Yet, though the youthful years are relatively few, they are none the less determining of the entire way of life of a newly married couple during their entire marriage. The road one takes in youth is the same one he will walk the rest of his life. The man who fails to lay out a smooth and level road during his youth, preferring to ramble up and down every hill and vale of pleasure, will in the end find that he has lost not only his youth but his every way in life.

True, it is more pleasant to ramble in youth than to walk on the main, well-traveled road. But what is one to do when youth passes, and one finds himself without any road at all? Then it is too late to begin. One has to be supernaturally strong, extraordinarily heroic, to renew his life during the "plateau years." Few people achieve it. Most men possess in middle age only those resources which they have prepared when they were at full strength.

In youth, however brief those years may really be, a man can maintain both his home and illicit pleasures. He may not feel any necessity of keeping to the main highway. The stormy passion of youth may bear him from place to place on their stormy waves. He seems to know only hours of pleasure, and these at frequent intervals. He rarely feels or sees the emptiness between those intervals. How easy for a young married couple to live under the delusion that they will be eternally happy!

But during the plateau years the hours of pleasure grow shorter and shorter. The emptiness between those hours continually widens. In contrast, the troubled hours lengthen and increase. The burden of life becomes ever heavier and more frightening. How banish the terror? How fill the void? Where find happiness?

One's feet are heavy, there is no path, no strength, the distance between the onset of the plateau years and old age stretches so long! Where can one find the love and affection to sustain one through that long trek?

VICTORY OF TRUE LOVE

There is a hidden treasure which, when found, can support a home forever, a well whose clear waters are an eternal blessing, yielding happiness and *Shalom Bayit*. The name of that treasure and that well is: esteem. He who esteems his friend will be loved by his friend — with a love that is true because it is not self-love. He who shows respect to his fellow-man will, in turn, be treated with respect. This esteem and respect will continually grow, enlarging into a love relatively still weak in youth, but growing stronger and stronger with the years.

Esteem does not spring up spontaneously. It is a plant that requires cultivation, effort, constant tending before its roots take hold in the hearts of men. The most suitable years for the cultivation of the sentiment of esteem are the years of youth — for youthful love allows a young couple to crown the heart's affection with respect.

The rule is: Say every word, do every deed that is a mark of respect both for the sayer and the one to whom it is said, the doer and the recipient; avoid any word, any act which is disrespectful to the sayer and the one to whom it is said, the doer and the recipient.

Everyone knows deep down in his heart just which deeds and words are dishonorable. Here is another general principle: Let every husband always think of himself as having married a princess, and treat her accordingly. Nor must he imagine that the esteem in which he holds his wife will ever lessen their love. To the contrary: respect will enhance their love.

THE ESSENCE OF ESTEEM

The essence of esteem is recognition of the value of the person esteemed.

We are bidden to respect ourselves because we are made in the image of God. Every virtue, every understanding that God implanted in Creation, He included in man. God gave man an upright posture, and gave him dominion over himself and the rest of God's handiwork. In the words of the Book of Psalms: "Yet Thou hast made him but little lower than the angels, and hast crowned him with glory and honor. Thou hast made him to have dominion over the deeds of Thy hands; all hast Thou placed under his feet." The dominion God gave man was the mark of the esteem in which He holds him. Man was also given the gift of eternal life — no other creature has an immortal soul. True, the body dies — but the spirit of man lives on in his children. All his deeds on earth leave their mark on his children. Thus did man's Creator clothe him with glory. Shall he shame that glory, through not esteeming his own worth and that of his wife?

For, as we have noted, man without woman is only half man, and woman without man is half woman. It is only when they are joined in marriage that they are complete. Without a wife a man does not in fact possess the dominion over the rest of creation that Psalms described.

Both husband and wife are obligated to respect the home they are building together. Every artisan respects the thing he makes — how much more ought those who form lives and produce a future generation to respect that which they are making! The fact is that man and wife in being father and mother are not only responsible for bringing life to the world. They must also nourish, sustain, raise, and educate their children, preparing them to accomplish all that they, in their turn, can accomplish. Through their children they make possible the continuation of the race. This is a role and an obligation deserving of the highest respect.

MARKS OF ESTEEM

The conventional mark of esteem is subordination. He who wishes to show his honor of another subordinates himself to him.

The man who respects himself will subordinate some of his desires to his total personality, using discipline and self-control. He will do or say nothing dishonorable — even though there be no one to observe. The husband who respects his wife will not lead her to do anything out of keeping with the esteem he wishes her to be held in. He will control his self-love in his relation with her.

The husband and wife who respect their home will keep out of improper speech, quarreling, contention — any thing that might lower its esteem. Order, discipline, cleanliness, purity — these shall pervade the Jewish home. Where esteem is, there is *Shalom Bayit*.

CHAPTER 11

■ FAITHFULNESS AND DEVOTION

■ Our sages declared: "Forty days before a child is conceived, the heavens proclaim: 'One that is the daughter of this and this man shall be married to one that is the son of this and this man.'" And when husband and wife enter the covenant of marriage, He who dwells on high joins their covenant, so to speak, and Himself confirms it. Should they violate that covenant, God, as a partner in it, requires redress both for the dishonor cast upon Him and on the covenant. Nor is the divine judgment tempered with compassion. For, in the words of Scripture, the penalty of this violation of the marriage covenant is: "that soul shall be cut off from his people" — the Torah prescribing that "both the adulterer and the adulteress shall surely be put to death" (after, due warning has been given and proper evidence of the adultery has been received.)

But, endless as is the punishment of those who violate the marriage covenant, equally endless is the reward of those who loyally keep it. Their two bodies become as one; their souls and hearts become as one; their lives flow from the same source. Such unity of heart and soul makes them fertile, giving birth to children who draw their living nourishment from the united roots of their parents' heart and soul.

Faithfulness and devotion are like two great lights that illuminate and purify the body. When these lights do not shine, the body is a dark and coarse sphere. Hence, physical cohabitation is permissible only where the hearts of husband and wife are as one; this alone distinguishes man from the beast. Without this genuine union, the act of cohabitation is in no way superior to the coupling of beasts, desecrating man's holiness, the holiness of the marriage covenant and of the Creator who Himself sanctified man and his passion in sanctifying the marriage covenant.

For that reason the Rabbis were strict in their prohibition of any relations which either husband or wife do not freely desire. The same prohibition applies if there is mutual desire but the mind is clouded (through fatigue, or intoxication, or sleepiness). Marital relations are most certainly prohibited if a divorce is being contemplated, or is in process. In all such instances, there is neither true faithfulness, nor love, nor spiritual union. Such cohabitation, where the body acts against the will of the spirit, is marred and repulsive.

When, however, a man and his wife are faithful and truly devoted to each other, prepared to sacrifice all for love of each other, where minds are unclouded, desire mutual, and the law permitting — relations between husband and wife are a pure and holy action, one where the body concludes the union of the souls. In the words of the Torah: "Therefore shall a man leave his father and his mother and shall cleave unto his wife, and they shall be one flesh" — one heart, one soul, and one flesh.

For the Creator has made it a natural thing for husband and wife to be more faithful to each other than they can ever be to any others — even their fathers and mothers who brought them into this world and reared them. Certainly, such faithfulness is stronger than loyalty to kin and to friends.

Why?

Because the loyalty of husband and wife to each other fills their life completely, body and soul. There is no aspect of human life which the loyalty of marriage does not encompass. All other loyalties, on the other hand, are limited to specific aspects of life.

Michal, the daughter of King Saul, is a symbol of that faithfulness.

Michal was a princess. Her father, a righteous man, loved her dearly. David was still unknown to fame, a man with many severe critics, under false suspicion. His character was as yet unrevealed, his righteousness unknown even to his wife, Michal. Persecuted by Michal's father, David's life hung by a hairbreadth. The common sentiment was that he would never escape Saul's anger. What was Michal to do? If she were to protect her husband, she might save him for the time being, but her father would forever be angry with her. In the end, David would be killed and Michal banished or worse. The temptation was great: Michal might easily hand over her husband, branded as a criminal, to her righteous father to receive his just punishment. By doing this, she could both save her princely honor and survive.

But Michal chose to save her husband, David. He was more beloved to her than her high-born honor — yes, more than her very life.

That is why Michal is the everlasting symbol of true faithfulness and devotion in marriage.

CHAPTER 12

■ ON BEING CONTENT WITH LITTLE

■ All men pursue wealth, but not all achieve it. Of those who do so, only a very few enjoy their wealth. For most people, the pursuit of riches never ceases. In the words of Scripture: "He that loveth silver shall not be satisfied with silver." Always avid for money, he wastes his life in the pursuit of the unattainable, never experiencing true joy.

Nor is that all. Eventually, in coveting that which belongs to others, he turns unethical. Stealing and cheating, he is filled with hatred of his fellow man. In his pursuit of money he deprives himself of the simple pleasures of life. He rises early, retires late, and cheats himself of precious hours of sleep. He is tense, worried, and fearful. His behavior evokes resentment, enmity, and strife. The home he builds is not the one God desires. For, in the words of the Torah: "Except the Lord build the house, they labor in vain that would built it" (Psalms 127).

What house *does* the Lord build? The very next psalm goes on to explain. "Happy is everyone that feareth the Lord, that walketh in His ways." "His ways" — meaning righteousness and justice, happiness and well-being. How does one achieve this state? "When thou eatest the labor of thy hands" — food that is the result of

87

thy labor, not that of others — "happy shalt thou be in this world" — happy with thy lot, neither impelled to sustain thyself with that which belongs to thy fellow man, nor envious to emulate him. Rather, live your own life, one that fits your taste. "And it shall go well with thee" in the Hereafter — for thou hast performed thy proper task on earth. Thou hast striven, thou hast eaten thy fill, hast uttered the blessing for the goodly portion the Lord thy God has given thee.

Not all men can achieve the wealth they desire. But all are capable of attaining true wealth — that which is a joy, which comes through righteousness, and is its master's due.

Such wealth is within the reach of the young couple starting out in marriage. The beginning of marriage determines its course. The newly-wed couple beginning to build a home can arrange their new life as they will. They are more open than other people. They have just begun to accept the difficult responsibilities of life. They have not yet been burned by life's fires. They are still open to love, can yearn purely for the good and the exalted, still dream with all their hearts of true happiness.

What obstacles stand in the way of the fulfillment of that dream?

A young couple can choose one of two paths. They can take the path that most people take, eyes closed — enslavement of body and soul. Or they can take the path chosen by persons of wisdom and sensibility — freedom in thought and deed.

Those who choose the first path simply act in imitation of their neighbors and acquaintances. It is not their own, their unique path, chosen because it suits them, and meets their own particular needs. It is marked by extreme effort and very little pleasures. Both husband and wife are slaves to work, yet there is barely enough income to cover expenses — they must go into debt merely to keep going. Too fatigued to engage in creative activity, real happiness and serenity are beyond them.

Their children, too, are denied genuine wealth — a father's lovingkindness, a mother's loving concern. They grow up poor in what really matters — the discipline and guidance of parents, for which there is no substitute. And when the children reach maturity, they are immediately drawn into the same vortex as their parents. The cycle repeats itself, like parents like children — the same flight from themselves and their own real needs, the same meaningless imitation of the lives of others.

But there is a second path in life, one which God has ordained, that is in total contrast to the first: the path we have described as one of freedom in deed and thought, which a man chooses of his own free will, exercising his own judgment.

Healthy search for the permanent joys of life. Body and soul each playing its proper part. Husband and wife playing their proper parts, not exchanging tasks and roles. A modest and balanced budget, with a modicum of savings. The home a place of rest, where the body can relax and the soul expand. Peaceful hours dedicated to the proper upbringing of children. Life that fits their needs and no one else's. Enjoyment of the fruits of their labor and the blessings God has bestowed on them in the manner prescribed by God. Being content with what they have, not covetous of their neighbors. This is the path of life.

Do not envy or compete with your neighbors. Their showy furniture, their modish clothing, their sumptuous table, their "superior" taste — all these have been bought with the suffering of themselves and their children, at the cost of serenity, well-being, and happiness. They have mortgaged body and soul for these luxuries — and they are not worth the price.

Why compete with your neighbors for wealth? Rather let them compete with you for happiness!

CHAPTER 13

■ HOSPITALITY

■ The Torah instructs us to begin building our world with acts of lovingkindness. For the Creator of the universe Himself founded His world on lovingkindness. In the words of Scripture: "The world is built on lovingkindness." God created the world for the good of His creatures and that they might act lovingly toward one another. God's first act toward Adam was one of benevolence — bringing Eve to Adam dressed as a bride. And, as we have noted above, God Himself attended the Chupah at the first wedding. Literally, lovingkindness was the first act of God in creation.

ABRAHAM

The father of the Jewish people, and of "a multitude of nations," also distinguished himself by lovingkindness. Abraham was kind to all men, without any ulterior motive — not even the high motive of persuading idolators to worship the one God. "Now the men of Sodom were .wicked and sinners against the Lord exceedingly." Nevertheless, Abraham did not hesitate to plead for mercy in their behalf. He did not use lovingkindness as a means for converting idolators; he used conversion as a means for increasing his benevolence. For the greatest kindness we can do for men who are created in the image of God is to bring them to a belief in Him. Hence, whenever the opportunity came his way, Abraham gave food and drink to idolators to sustain their bodies, and taught them wisdom, understanding, and knowledge of God to sustain their souls. Nor did Abraham deny food and drink to those who were poor and empty of soul, incapable of receiving the perfect lovingkindness of belief in God.

A HOME IS BUILT ON LOVINGKINDNESS

In time past our forefathers, the children of Abraham, preceded the wedding feast with a feast for the poor — in keeping with the dictum: "To make the poor rejoice is the beginning of joy." The new home was to be founded on lovingkindness. With this practice our forefathers were saying to their children, as it were: "Today we parents tender you a feast after we have feasted the poor. Tomorrow you will be making your own feasts — learn from us, and invite the needy to your table that your feasts may be pleasing to God." At the beginning of each marriage comes lovingkindness.

OPEN YOUR DOORS

With marriage you build a new home. This is now your private domain. Still, do not shut the doors of your home tight. "Let your doors be opened wide." If learned men wish to use your home as a meeting place to discuss communal needs — open your doors and let them in. If friends and relatives invite you to join in their happiness or wish to join in yours — open your doors and let them in. If people wish to solicit your help for charity or other public causes — open your doors and let them in. All causes that enhance the' individual or public weal are the proper concern of the home; they have a place in your private life. In the tree of mankind every individual branch depends for its life on the vitality of the tree as a whole. The death of any branch is a danger signal to every other branch. Conversely, the health of each individual branch contributes to the health of all the other branches.

But shut the doors of your home to mischief-makers, plotters, conspirators. For you are bidden to open your doors to the lovers of mankind, not to those who would destroy it.

"And make the poor members of your household" — they are to be more than mere visitors or guests — the poor are to be "members of the household." You should be as concerned for the poor as you are for your household. Think of the poor both at home and abroad, as you think of your household. For the poor man actually helps the master of the home more than the master helps him — by securing divine blessing.

THE SAGES ON HOSPITALITY

Said Rabbi Elazar: "Hospitality is a greater thing than all the sacrificial offerings put together, for Scripture says: To do righteousness and justice is more acceptable to the Lord than sacrifice." (Tractate Succah 69).

Said Rabbi Avin: "God stands at the right hand of the poor man standing at your door, for Scripture says: 'Because He standeth at the right hand of the needy.' If you give to the poor man, be it known to you that He who stands at his right hand will give you your reward. If you do not, be it known to you that He who stands at the poor man's right hand will exact payment from you." (Vayikra Rabbah ch. 34).

It is preferable to share a meal at one's own table with the poor than to give money. The first is a personal act, the second an impersonal one. A meal is of immediate benefit; in the case of money, the poor man's benefit is delayed until he has bought something with the money.

When the scribe Ezra went up to the Land of Israel from Babylonia, bringing the first returnees from the Exile with him, he issued ten edicts. One of these ten was: "Bake bread on Friday for the whole week, that there may be bread for the poor." (Jerusalem Talmud, Tractate Megilah, ch. 4).

"My son, take care to show respect to the poor. Speak gently to the poor man, and commiserate with him in his troubles. Give him alms privately. Feed him in your own home. Do not watch him eating. For he is famished, and your look may embarrass him." (From Rabbi Eliezer the Great's testament to his son.)

"Teach your household humility — so that if a poor man stands at the door and asks: 'Is father in?,' they will respond: 'Yes, come in.' As soon as the poor man enters, let the table be set for him." (Avot of Rabbi Nathan, chap. 7).

"Rabbi Joshua said: 'If a poor man comes to you in the morning, help him. If a poor man comes in the evening, help him. For you do not know for which of the two men God has prescribed your help — perhaps both men are equally deserving.' " (Bereshit Rabbah ch. 61).

"Shammai said: 'Greet all persons cordially. For if a man give his fellow even the richest gifts in the world, but with a morose face, the Torah considers that gift to be as nothing. But he who greets his fellow man cordially, even if he has nothing to give him, is considered to have given the finest gift of all." (Avot 1; Avot of Rabbi Nathan 13).

Do not show a poor man a dour face when you give him alms, lest he imagine you are giving charity under duress. Though something troubles you, take care to smile, and conceal your trouble. (Maimonides, The Laws of Charity).

Rabbenu Yonah wrote: "When a poor man visits you at home, receive him cordially, and serve him food at once, for sometimes he will not have eaten for some time and be ashamed to ask for food. . . . Console and encourage him. Attend to the poor man's needs yourself, even if you have many servants. Is any of us superior to Abraham, who served the disguised angels with his own hands?"

FRAUDS

There are frauds who, pretending to be poor, ask for charity. One ought not refuse assistance to any man who holds out his hand. Nobody is so wise that he can tell at a glance the difference between the truly poor man and the fraud. If anything, the fraud is more likely to win sympathy under questioning. So consider everyone who asks for your help as deserving.

Besides, the sages teach us to be grateful to the deceivers — if it were not for them, we should never fulfill our obligations to the poor. For, however much one gives to a poor man, one is always uneasy lest it is not enough. But knowing that some who pretend to be poor are really frauds, we feel that we can discharge our obligation with a small gift. Hence, even if you suspect the applicant for charity of not being deserving, treat him respectfully, and do not turn him away empty-handed.

A fortiori, one must not embarrass a poor man by referring to the fact that he lives off charity and has no other occupation. Every man has his private reasons. The man may seem healthy enough, but not really be so; he may seem able to find work, but really not be able to. In any event, one must not shame him. To embarrass a poor man is to harm oneself. As the sages said in the Midrash: "Scripture says: 'The rich and the poor meet together — the Lord is the Maker of them all.' (Proverbs 22). The poor man says to the rich man: 'Help me.' If the rich man does not help him – then 'the Lord is the Maker of them all' – He who made the poor man poor, can make him rich as well, and He who made the rich man rich can make him poor as well. If the rich man says to the poor man: 'Why do you not work and eat of the fruit of your labor? See how full your thighs are, how strong your body!' – God says to him: 'You not only give the poor man nothing of what belongs to you, but you look with an evil eye on that which I gave him!' – Therefore – 'If he hath begotten a son, there is nothing in his hand' (Ecclesiastes 5). Of all the riches man has, he will leave nothing to his son." (Vayikrah Rabbah 34 and Midrash Ecclesiastes 5).

Rabbi Yehudah said in the name of Rav: "Hospitality shown to visiting strangers is even greater than hospitality shown to the Divine Presence. For it is said: And he [Abraham] said: My lord, if now I have found favor in thy sight, pass not away, I pray thee, from thy servant.'" (Tractate Sabbath 127).

HOSPITALITY TO THE RICH

The mitzvah of hospitality extends to the rich as well as the poor. There are times when a man will arrive at a place where he has no acquaintances; even if he has money, that may not help to find a proper place to stay. Or he may not be used to eating and sleeping in a public establishment, being at ease only with persons who make him feel at home. Look after such a visitor as you would a poor man, for in respect to his unmet needs, he too is poor.

On the other hand, since people vary widely in character and habit, always behave toward your visitor so as to please him, not yourself. As the sages have said: "Do not press your guest to eat if he prefers not to" (Chulin 94). By pressing your guest to do as you wish, besides imposing on him you are being deceitful. You are putting him under an obligation for a "kindness" you know in advance he will not enjoy. Rather, the host should say: "The table is set. Help yourself to as much as you want of whatever you want. In my home, your pleasure is my pleasure." There is no room for self-pride on the part of the host in the mitzvah of hospitality.

■ THE PRACTICE OF CHARITY

1. *It is a positive commandment to give charity to the poor if the giver can afford it.*

2. *Everyone who sees a poor man ask for charity and pretends not to notice him, transgresses a prohibition of the Torah.*

3. *We are commanded to give the poor man whatever he needs. If he has no garment we are to clothe him. If he has no home, we are to provide him with one.*

4. *If a poor man whom one does not know says, "I am hungry, give me food!" one does not check whether he is a deceiver but gives him food immediately. If he is unclad and asks for clothing, one does check after him. But if one knows him, one clothes him immediately in appropriate clothing.*

5. *One is not obliged to give a poor man who goes around begging, a large contribution, but it is forbidden to send him away emtpy-handed.*

6. *A woman takes precedence over a man with respect to food, clothing, and redemption from captivity.*

7. *One must be more careful with respect to charity than with any other commandment, for charity is one of the signs of our lineage from Abraham our forefather.*

8. *A man never becomes poor through giving charity, nor does any harm or evil befall him because of it.*

9. *One who gives no charity is called evil, (as an idol-worshipper), a sinner, a wicked man. The Holy One Blessed be He heeds the cry of the poor, as it is said: "Thou hearest the cry of the poor." Therefore one ought to heed the cry of the poor.*

CHAPTER 14

■ RELATIVES AND NEIGHBORS

■ Though providing for the poor is a great mitzvah, it should not take the place of, or diminish, one's charitable efforts in behalf of relatives and neighbors. In charity, kin and neighbors take precedence — this is a basic principle of the mitzvah. As the book Menorat Hamaor puts it: "What should one do who has food left over to distribute as charity? Let him first provide for his parents; then his brothers and sisters; then his neighbors. Finally, if there is still a surplus, let him extend his charity to others. As Scripture says: 'And bring the poor that are cast out to thy house.' " (Isaiah 58).

SELFISHNESS

Even if a person is liberal with his charity, if he does not invite his poor relatives to share in his celebrations, he is considered cruel and selfish. And no person is more hateful to God than the selfish one.

Certainly, God who loves the poor could feed them with liberality Himself. Why, then, does He make them dependent on the rich for bread? God does so deliberately — bringing together a poor man who may need to be forgiven for some past misdeed and a rich man who requires divine mercy. When the poor man extends his hand to the rich man for charity, his sins are erased through the shame to which the changed color of his face testifies, the anguish of being reduced to begging. When the wealthy man responds with compassion to the poor man's plea, God at once has compassion on him. In this way, the act of charity has been meritorious for the poor man and the rich. This is particularly true of charity given to relatives. The man who is genuinely merciful will feel greater compassion for the suffering of his relatives than for any other persons. They are, after all, his own flesh and blood, to be regarded almost as his children. And no natural father is unmoved by the poverty of a good and deserving son, no natural father drives such a son away because he is ashamed of his son's need.

He who gives charity to poor relatives but is ashamed of them is not really merciful; there is too much haughty condescension connected with his charity. He is acting out of pride in his wealth and contempt of their poverty, wishing to maintain the recipients of his aid in a state of embarrassment and abject inferiority. He is selfish in that he wishes to keep the poor dependent on him for their livelihood. He has no desire to help them recover their dignity. His callousness extends even to his own flesh and blood.

The selfish benefactor deceives himself if he thinks to win people's respect with his grudging charity. They may flatter him to his face — but in their heart of hearts they hate him, for everyone can recognize selfishness, however disguised. The poor man would be better advised to exhaust every other alternative rather than seek assistance from those who are selfish.

NEIGHBORS

Relatives take priority in charity; next come neighbors.

Whom do people consider to be a friendly person? One who is considerate of both neighbors and strangers. But even if one is not particularly cordial with strangers, if one maintains good relations with one's neighbors, one is considered a decent human being. In the words of the Ethics of the Fathers: "What is the good way? Rabbi Yosi said: 'The way of a good neighbor.'"

A good neighbor is one who is friendly, avoids conflict, is always ready with a prompt hello and a hearty smile, welcomes company, is aware of the sorrows of others and offers assistance.

But the neighbor who is always quarrelsome, bears tales, is aloof, uninterested in other people's troubles and indifferent to their joys — is disliked and should be avoided. The smiling face he may show to strangers is all too often motivated by self-interest, or by the desire to win public approval.

So one ought to make an effort to be on good terms with neighbors, whether or not they can help one or come of similar background. One ought to feel to one's neighbors something of that affection and sense of obligation one feels toward relatives.

CHAPTER 15

■ KINDNESS TO ANIMALS

■ People are to be judged by their treatment of animals as by their behavior toward humans — for they too are God's creatures. This is particularly true of domesticated beasts and birds.

It is forbidden us to cause unnecessary pain to any living creature, whether or not we own it. We may take the life of a living thing for purposes of food or self-protection. But the Torah prohibits us from inflicting pain on any living creature for any other purpose. Nor may we cause a living creature anguish in any manner. For since everything that God created He created for His glory, the honor of all of His creatures is precious to Him.

Consequently, parents must train their children not to inflict pain on living creatures — whether these be domestic or wild, big or small. He who causes a living creature to suffer, to gratify his own perverse pleasure is violating a prohibition in the Torah; he is also brutalizing himself, spreading suffering, suppressing compassion and mercy.

One ought particularly to be on guard against inflicting pain on the beasts or birds he raises at home for pleasure or use. A Jewish home should be the scene of compassion, not of deliberate suffering.

Our sages have urged us to avoid cruelty to animals in numerous admonitions.

"One should not adopt an animal, beast, or bird, unless he has prepared food for it in advance." (Jerusalem Talmud Ketuboth, ch. 4).

"Rabbi Yehudah said in the name of Rav: 'One ought not eat before feeding one's animal,' for Scripture says first, 'And I will give grass in thy fields for thy cattle' — and then it says, 'and thou shalt eat and be satisfied.'" (Berachot 40).

The sensitive person will develop his own safeguards to prevent pain or suffering to any living creature sheltered in his home.

■ CHAPTER 16

■ SANCTIFYING THE ACT OF EATING

■ Once your animals have been fed, and you have shared your bread with those who are hungry, having guests at your table, you may be seated and eat — your table is pure, your food sanctified. Wash your hands (as an act of consecration), utter the blessing before eating, eat, and utter the blessing after eating.

SANCTIFICATION

One is required to wash his hands twice at each meal, once before eating and once after — or, as the rabbis phrased it, to perform "first waters" and "last waters." This commandment has not only a hygienic reason — though that alone would have sufficed. But, like all God's commandments, the washing of the hands before and after eating has a symbolic meaning — it signifies the purity of the soul and the sanctification of man's aspiring spirit. This is evident from the fact that one is required to clean and dry one's hands before "first waters."

The ritual of first and last waters is a richly allusive one. When a Jew sits down to eat, he cleans his hands and holds them palm up, as though to testify that his hands are unsullied by any act of robbery or deceit performed to make his meal possible. Then again, his hands are open to the poor who are hungry. They are with him at his table, or he has enabled them to eat at their own table. Such cleanliness of hands, signifying purity of soul, is not achieved lightly. Many are the tests a man must pass, many the temptations he must overcome, before he can consider his hands truly clean, his enjoyment of the food he has labored to earn, pure.

Having eaten your fill, make sure that your own full stomach does not lead you to forget the continuing needs of others, those who are still hungry. As the Torah says: "Jeshurun [Israel] waxed fat and kicked" — indifference to the wants of others is a universal danger. Though the meal be prepared according to the commandments of ritual purity, its after effect can be defilement of the innermost soul. For a full stomach often, so to speak, coats the heart with fat, hardening the sensibilities, producing self-centeredness, a concentration on sensuality. Hence we are bidden to perform the act of "second waters," washing our hands after the meal as a reminder of our continuing need for purification — from the defilement which even ritually pure food can produce.

"First waters" require the use of a certain specified amount of water, carefully measured; "second waters" do not. For the purpose of "first waters" is to remind us that we are bidden always to strive for purity in the preparation of our food — according to the "measure" of our capacity. "Second waters" remind us that, after all our efforts, when all is said and done, we need Divine help; that even acts which are permitted us may lead to self-defilement. Having done our best, we must still pray: "Create a pure heart in me, O God!" "Second waters" allude symbolically to the waters of purification that come from Heaven, from heights which the hand of man cannot reach. Hence, in the final analysis, purification is a gift from heaven. He who sanctifies himself as best as he can on earth, however little it be in the sight of heaven, is sanctified by heaven, with a sanctification that cannot be measured — hence "second waters" require no specific measure of water.

■ WASHING THE HANDS BEFORE MEALS

1.   *Only if one eats bread over which one pronounces the blessing "He who brings forth bread from the earth," is one obliged to wash one's hands ritually before eating.*

2.   *One should pour water on one's hands from a cup or glass which is not crushed or chipped; its rim should be smooth and without grooves.*

3.   *The cup or class should be one normally used for liquids and should contain at least 86 ccs. Other authorities require a minimum of 120 ccs.*

4.   *Before washing all rings should be removed, and all dirt or stains should be removed from the hands.*

5.   *The water used for washing should be drinkable water not previously used for other purposes.*

6.   *The water should be poured by manual effort on the hands. For this reason simply opening a narrow tap is not proper. A wide tap is permissible on condition that one opens and closes the tap for each jet of water poured on the hands.*

7.   *One may also immerse one's hands in a river or a natural spring or in a "mikveh" instead of washing them in the usual way.*

8.   *If one washes one's hands in the usual way, a minimum of 86 ccs. (or 120 ccs. — see above) should be poured from the container in a single pouring, so as to cover the fingers and palm up to the wrist of each hand. After the first pouring, each hand should be washed a second time, with more water from the container. There are some who wash each hand three times.*

9.   *Care should be taken not to touch the unwashed hand with the hand already washed and still wet. Similarly a man*

who has not yet washed his hands should not touch the hands of someone who has washed but has not yet dried his hands. If this happens, washing should be repeated.

10. *After washing both one's hands in the proper manner, the hands should be rubbed together while still wet. Then, raising the tips of the fingers upwards towards the head, one should recite the blessing: "Blessed art Thou, o Lord, King of the universe, who has sanctified us with His commandments, and commanded us concerning the washing of hands." The hands should then be thoroughly dried before eating.*

11. *If one has a bandage on one's hand, one need only wash the uncovered parts of that hand.*

12. *The blessing should be recited immediately after the washing of the hands, without any interruption.*

TABLE MANNERS

One should not serve food or drink in unclean containers. Nor should one taste or sip out of containers and then pass them on to others.

One should not treat food disrespectfully or throw food from place to place. One should not sit on a box of dates or figs or any other fruit. And food should not be used as a support or as a lid. (Sofrim 3.)

One should not talk while eating. This could be dangerous, for food could enter the windpipe. (Taanith 5.)

Table manners are sometimes founded on health factors. But in addition to this, we must remember that the eating of food forms part of a life dedicated to the service of God. It is therefore itself part of God's worship. For this reason the Jewish table is likened to the altar on which sacrifices to God are brought. When you eat your meals, you are seated before the Holy One Blessed be He. See to it, therefore, that your behavior should find favor in His sight.

■ CHAPTER 17

■ PRIVATE AND PUBLIC DOMAIN

■ Though a man's home is his castle where he may do as he pleases, he is obliged to take care lest any possession of his cause injury to a neighbor or passer-by. The sages said: "One may not keep a wild dog or put up a faulty ladder — for the Torah teaches us: 'That thou bring not blood upon thy house.'" (Tractate Baba Kama 15).

A wild dog's bark and very appearance is terrifying, often endangering the security of passers-by. The only valid ground for keeping a wild dog is for protection. But even then the dog should be kept under guard, so as not to inflict injury. As the Talmud teaches us: "Raising a bad dog in one's home is like breeding a pig there. The same curse applies to the dog as to the pig: 'Cursed be the man who breeds pigs.'" (Baba Kama 83).

"One may not put up a faulty ladder in his courtyard" — lest outsiders, unaware of the danger, climb the ladder and be hurt.

We are also bidden to prevent smoke and foul odors from escaping from our property into the public domain. The same is true of loud noises at all times, music and singing when neighbors are asleep. We may not engage in any activity even in our own courtyard which a passer-by would find distasteful.

It goes without saying that we ought not to throw garbage into the public domain. It is forbidden to dirty up a public place or to place any obstacle in it. We are obliged to be as concerned with the cleanliness of public property as we are with our own.

"The rabbis taught: 'In ancient days pious men buried thorns and splinters three handbreadths deep in their fields so that plows would not be damaged or bring the thorns and splinters to the surface.' " (Baba Kama 30.)

Another text teaches us that we ought not to throw stones from our private property into the public domain. Once a pious man came across a man doing just that. The pious man said: "Fool! Why do you remove stones from the public domain and throw them into yours?!" The man made fun of him. But in the course of time the stone-thrower was forced to sell his field. Once, walking in what had become a public domain, he stumbled over one of the very stones he had thrown there. Said he: "How right that pious man was who said to me: 'Why do you throw stones from the public domain into yours?!' " (Baba Kama 50).

The moral is: Regard the public domain as belonging equally to you, for you are one of the public — and treat it with the same respect as you treat your own property.

We are forbidden to hoard large amounts of food; the result is food shortage and rising prices. The hoarder harms himself, as well as earning the resentment of others.

This is particularly true in times of famine and distress. Every surplus piece of food a man hoards, he is taking out of the mouth of another person who needs it. (Baba Bathra 90).

We are enjoined to work for community betterment, identifying ourselves with the public interest through personal effort as well as with material aid, for the needs of the community are the sum of the needs of the individuals who comprise the community. Personal interest dictates our participation in community efforts; today other people may need a particular service, not we; tomorrow we, not they. How can we expect others to join us in providing for our future needs if we do not cooperate with them in providing for theirs?

But even if we are certain that we will never need the help of others, we are still obligated to cooperate with them in meeting the communal needs. Everyone derives some benefit from the community — though it be nothing more than companionship. Would it be fair to accept a benefit from the community without sharing the common burden? Consequently, at times a man is under an obligation to allow the public to share the benefit of his possessions, by permitting the public to trespass on his property, for example.

As Rabbi Yosef said in the name of Rabbi Judah: "One ought not to pour out the water from his well unused, if others need it." (Yebamoth 11).

"If a man does not permit others to pass through his fields (as a short-cut or for pleasure), though the crop be already harvested, people may well say of him: 'What pleasure can that afford him? What injury do people do to him?!' The verse applies to him: 'Withhold not good from him to whom it is due, when it is in the power of thy hand to do it.' (Proverbs 3)." According to Maimonides, it was wise Solomon who decreed that "travelers may walk through the paths of the fields" (Maimonides, The Laws Pertaining to Monetary Damages, ch. 5). Traditions tells us that when Joshua settled the tribes in the land of Canaan, he did it on condition that they act generously with one another. Hence the ancient Jewish obligation of mutual responsibility for the community welfare.

■ A PROTECTIVE FENCE

1.   *The Torah commands a man to build a parapet round his roof, whether the house belongs to him or whether he is merely a tenant. The verse reads (Deut. 22, 8): "When thou buildest a new house, then thou shalt make a parapet for thy roof, that thou bring not blood upon thy house, if a man fall from thence."*

2.   *Similarly, one is required to build railings alongside steps leading upwards, and to build a fence round a pit or well in one's property, or cover them with a cover strong enough to support the weight of men or animals who walk over.*

3.   *The height of the parapet or fence should be ten "tefachim" (which is about 39 inches), and the parapet or fence should be strong enough for a man to be able to lean on it without it falling.*

4.   *Any roof higher from the ground than 81 centimeters of an area not less than 2 meters by 2 meters, requires a parapet.*

5.   *Before installing the parapet, one recites the blessing: Blessed art Thou, o Lord our God, King of the Universe, who hath sanctified us with his commandments and commanded us to make a parapet."*

CHAPTER 18

■ THE MEZUZAH

■ The mezuzah attached to the doorpost of every Jewish home is like the royal emblem engraved at a palace entrance. For a Jewish home, being the place where the Divine Presence dwells, is the residence of true royalty. The children born and reared in this home are there educated to live lives dedicated to Torah and divinely ordained works. The everyday behavior of its inhabitants, the very business they transact — all are permeated by a spirit of mercy and lovingkindness. In the same spirit food and drink are offered freely to all who enter. And it is the mezuzah on the door which testifies to the special quality of the Jewish home — that "God dwells in this house."

With the mezuzah, the members of this household reject any claim to success by their own efforts; rather, this is their declaration that whatever they own is due to the Lord. It is their hope that He whose Name rests on this home will preserve its inhabitants from sin and retribution, bestowing a spirit of brotherly love and peace on them.

Wherever Jews live, the mezuzah is an identifying mark for their wandering brethren. Travelers far from home, at the sight of a mezuzah, are reassured — they have found co-religionists, and are among their own.

What is written in the mezuzah? It contains passages from Deuteronomy 6:4-9 and 11:13-21, written on parchment in twenty-two lines according to the same rules as those for the Torah and Tephillin. It begins with the Shema, the Unification of God's Name, and continues as follows:

"HEAR, O ISRAEL: THE LORD OUR GOD, THE LORD IS ONE. And thou shalt love the Lord thy God with all thy heart, and with all thy soul, and with all thy might. And these words, which I command thee this day, shall be upon thy heart; and thou shalt read them diligently unto thy children, and shalt talk of them when thou sittest in thy house, and when thou walkest by the way, and when thou liest down, and when thou risest up. And thou shalt bind them for a sign upon thy hand, and they shall be for frontlets between thine eyes. And thou shalt write them upon the door-posts of thy house, and upon thy gates.

"And it shall come to pass, if ye shall hearken diligently unto My commandments which I command you this day, to love the Lord your God, and to serve Him with all your heart and with all your soul, that I will give the rain of your land in its season, the former rain and the latter rain, that thou mayest gather in thy corn, and thy wine, and thine oil. And I will give grass in thy fields for thy cattle, and thou shalt eat and be satisfied. Take heed to yourselves, lest your heart be deceived, and ye turn aside, and serve other gods, and worship them; and the anger of the Lord be kindled against you, and He shut up the heaven, so that there shall be no rain, and the ground shall not yield her fruit; and ye perish quickly from off the good land which the Lord giveth you. Therefore shall ye lay up these My words in your heart and in your soul; and ye shall bind them for a sign upon your hand, and they shall be for frontlets between your eyes. And ye shall teach them to your children, talking of them, when thou sittest in thy house, and when thou walkest by the way, and when thou liest down, and when thou risest up. And thou shalt write them upon the door-posts of thy house, and upon thy gates; that your days may be multiplied, and the days of your children, upon the land which the Lord swore unto your fathers to give them, as the days of the heavens above the earth."

Traditionally, the mezuzah is thought of as protecting the Jewish home from harm. But we do not fix the mezuzah to the doorpost of our homes for security sake — as a kind of charm, or amulet. Maimonides has explained the purpose of the mezuzah: "One should be very sure to fix a mezuzah to the doorpost of one's home, for the commandment to do so is an obligation that falls upon all of us, and at all times. Whenever the Jew enters or leaves his home, confronted by the proclamation of God's oneness, he is reminded to love Him. Faced with this reminder, he will be roused from lethargy and indulgence in temporary vanities, realizing that nothing but the love of God is eternal. At once he will be recalled to the path of righteousness. As our sages have said: 'Every man who bears Tephillin on forehead and arm, and fringes on his garment, and whose doorpost bears a mezuzah, is saved from sin.' For these are the angels who protect him from sin, as it is written (Psalms 34:8): 'The angel of the Lord encampeth round about them that fear Him and delivereth them.'" (Maimonides, Hilchot Mezuzah, chapter 6.)

■ SOME RULES CONCERNING MEZUZAH

1. *Every door to any house or room, balcony, porch, or hall, whether in a home or an office, a factory, workshop, cellar, storage-room or attic, and similarly every gate in front of a stair-hallway, or yard, or city entrance, through which people enter and go out, even if only on rare occasions, requires a mezuzah. However the door or gate must consist of two doorposts and a lintel.*

2. *A room used for more personal or unclean purposes, such as a bathroom, lavatory, etc. is not to have a mezuzah on its doorpost.*

3. *An opening to a cellar or to a roof, the doorposts and door of which are not vertical but horizontal, is exempt from a mezuzah.*

4. *A "succah" (tabernacle) or any other shack built only for temporary use, which will later be demolished, is exempt from a mezuzah.*

5. *In a new house in which the doors have not yet been hinged, the hinging of the doors should be done first and only thereafter should the mezuzah be affixed to each doorpost.*

6. *When affixing the mezuzah, it should be folded from end to beginning wrapped in paper or a container, and the following blessing should be recited: "Blessed art Thou, o Lord our God, King of the Universe, who sanctified us with His commandments and commanded us to affix the mezuzah." Then the mezuzah is attached by nails to the right hand doorpost as one enters.*

7. *Care should be taken not to perforate the parchment with the nails. The nails should be knocked through the container of the mezuzah only.*

112

8.   *One blessing will suffice for the affixing of several mezuzot at the same time.*

9.   *The mezuzah should be placed at the beginning of the upper third of the height of the doorpost, and on the right-hand doorpost as one enters. It should be placed in an inclined position with the top pointing inwards and the bottom pointing outwards.*

10.   *In the event of the door being very tall, the mezuzah should be fixed at the level of the shoulder of the average man.*

11.   *If the mezuzah has been affixed below the upper third of an average doorpost, or below the height of an average man's shoulder in the case of a very tall doorpost; if it has been simply suspended without being affixed — if it has been affixed to the wrong doorpost — then in all these cases it is as if a mezuzah had not been affixed at all; in which case, the mezuzah must be re-affixed properly.*

12.   *Not only an owner but also a tenant in a house is obliged to affix a mezuzah. For the affixing of the mezuzah is the duty of whoever lives in the house.*

13.   *A person entering a new house must affix a mezuzah within 30 days (in Israel he must affix it immediately).*

14.   *When leaving an apartment, whose new tenant will be a Jew, one is forbidden to remove the mezuzah and to take it with him. If the mezuzah is an expensive one, one is entitled to demand that the new tenant pay for it. If the new tenant is a non-Jew, it is permissible to remove the mezuzah in order to avoid its desecration.*

15.   *The mezuzah of a house should be checked by an expert every three years in order to see that nothing has happened to invalidate them.*

CHAPTER 19

■ CHALLAH, TERUMOTH AND MAASROTH
(The Dough Offering, Heave Offerings and Tithes)

■ A people is praised which acknowledges its blessings with gratitude, but woe the people which is ungrateful!

Many are the kindnesses which God bestowed upon Israel.
Correspondingly, the debt which Israel owes to God is a large one.
But though the Jewish people is unable to repay its debt entirely, all
the same it is not an ungrateful people. It does not fail to acknowl-
edge the goodness of its Benefactor. How? With the Mitzvoth of
Offerings and Tithes.

CHOSEN

The people of Israel is a chosen people; a people selected by
God from among all other peoples to serve as a kingdom of priests
and a holy nation, as the most exalted of the nations of the Earth.

Israel's Torah is chosen. Before the depths were fashioned, before
mountains were formed, before Earth and civilization were wrought
— the Torah was God's treasured possession. The Torah served as
God's blueprint for the creation of the world. Those who study its
teachings, uncover the mysteries of existence and become partners
to their Creator. But, neither to angels was it given, nor to the
nations. To Israel alone was the Torah given.

The land of Israel is chosen, as is written: "For God chose Zion. He desired it as a dwelling place for Himself" (Psalm 132). It was a land which flowed with milk and honey; in whose valleys and hills there flowed streams and well-springs. It was a land of wheat and barley and vines ———, a land which lacked for nothing, whose stones were iron and from whose mountains copper was to be hewn, a land of hills and valleys watered by the heavens, a land sought by God, a land upon which the eyes of God rest from the beginning of the year to the end of the year.

The matter may be compared to the parable of a king who had a son more beloved than his other sons, and a vineyard more fruitful than all his other vineyards. Said he: "I will give the most precious of my vineyards to the most beloved of my sons." Let Israel, the chosen of peoples, inherit the land which is chosen among lands.

Not like all lands is this one. All other lands sometimes sustain their inhabitants, and sometimes not. But never do they depart from the laws of nature. This land is at times blessed and at times cursed — but it is always ruled by a force beyond nature. When blessed, its blessing is bountiful even after little seeding; even a little of its food nourishes greatly. When it is not blessed nothing avails to open its treasures. For its prosperity does not depend on labor and toil but rather on — "the blessing (will come) if you obey the mitzvoth of the Lord your God, and the curse if you will not obey" (Deuteronomy 11).

Perhaps you will say, where is the blessing of the land today?

This is its greatness and this its blessing, that despite the curse resting upon it so long, it still brings forth fruit. The Lord has not yet visited his people with a complete remembrance, and for thousands of years its enemies have diligently sought to destroy it and to increase its desolation. And yet even now — how sweet are its fruits, how sweet its air; How great are the majesty and the beauty destined for the land when God's complete remembrance will come to it, (soon in our days); when the land will light up its face to all its returning sons. This land was a chosen land; it will remain a chosen land unto eternity.

CHOSEN BUT NOT HAUGHTY

A people which is chosen, whose Torah is chosen and whose land is chosen, may become proud and forget the God who delivered it from bondage. It may say in its heart: "With the strength of my hand and with my wisdom did I achieve all this. Greatness and honor and glory are mine!"

Heaven forbid, should the heart of this people become thus conceited — evil and bitter will its end be. "The Lord hates all who are proud of heart"; all who are proud of heart — even such as are truly great in achievement. For God has sworn that He would cast down the conceited to earth, even if they should rise to the heavens.

BETWEEN KOHANIM (PRIESTS) AND MASTERS

God did not make of His people a people of masters but "a kingdom of Kohanim". What is the difference between masters and Kohanim? Both are honored; but while masters refrain from work and are served by their servants, the honor of Kohanim resides in their service to others. Their glory lies in the fulfillment of their mission. The service they are bidden to perform is a sacred one. They are messengers sent for the purpose of achieving atonement, purification and blessing for their people and for the whole world. Kohanim are exalted only through the sanctity of their service and the glory of their senders.

Israel has an exalted task amongst the nations of the world — to be a light unto the nations, to draw the nations near to their Creator till all the world's inhabitants will acknowledge the sovereignty of God alone. Even if the people of Israel does not achieve its task completely, it remains a protective fence for the world, and prevents the world from sinking in its impurities. The Prophets of Israel and the mass of its people stand in every age as a banner unto the nations and remind them that there is a God of Judgement on earth. Conceit is therefore not fitting for Israel, for conceit is the source of every defilement. Rather is modesty fitting for Israel; the modesty of subjection to God, who granted Israel exaltation.

If Israel, the chosen amongst nations, ascribes its glory to the King of Glory, then all the world's peoples are led to similarly glorify Him — as well as the people of Israel which honors Him. And all the world is thereby brought to perfection. But if Israel, which is the Kohen amongst the nations, betrays its mission, takes glory unto itself, and renders service for the sake of its own glory — then all the peoples of the earth become ascendant over Israel, and the people of Kohanim becomes the most degraded of peoples.

A REMEMBRANCE OF MISSION

Many mitzvoth were given to Israel as reminders of its intended mission; as preventives of conceit and ingratitude. The mitzvoth of setting aside heave offerings, tithes and dough offerings are amongst these. As long as Israel observed these mitzvoth, blessing rested on its land and a crown of glory was worn by all the land's inhabitants. When Israel forsook these mitzvoth and ceased to observe them, blessing departed from the land; the crown was lifted from Israel's head, and in the place of earlier exaltation, it now knew the pain of degradation.

THE TRIBE OF LEVI — THE TITHE OF THE TRIBES TO GOD

Israel's hosts came out of the Egyptian house of bondage with outstretched arm; and with outstretched arm did they come to the sacred boundaries of the land of their inheritance. Their King, who had driven nations before them, was at their head. Ten tribes took possession of the land. But only nine of the tribes were allotted sections of the land for possession. One tribe received no portion in the land — the tribe of Levi — which was consecrated to God. (The remaining two and a half tribes settled on the eastern side of the Jordan.)

What reason was there for a human tithe; for the giving of a "tithe of the tribes"?

The reason is easily grasped. For, when the people of Israel settled in the land, its individual members were each immersed in material concerns. One was busy building a home while another was busy in his field. One attended his vineyard; another, his garden. The newly settled land was beloved, the work it required was great. Effort expended on it was holy. It demanded the total energies of its new owners. What was to become of Torah? When would the people find time to immerse themselves in the study of Torah and to perform the tasks of their Divinely appointed mission?

At the time of seeding, they would be required to plant seeds. At the time of ploughing, they were to plough. At the time of reaping, they were to reap. All the same, the people as a whole was not to forsake its sacred mission; even as its individual members were each engaged in material pursuits.

One of its tribes, the tribe of Levi, was not to be given an allocation of land. The remaining tribes were to acquire Levi's intended fields and vineyards, and were to tend them as their own. When the land would yield its produce, they were to share its fruit with the dispossessed members of the tribe of Levi. They were to bring of its first fruits to the sanctuary in Jerusalem, and to present them to the Kohanim then in attendance. They were also to present heave offerings from the ingathered produce to the Kohanim (not then on duty) living elsewhere in the land of Israel. They were to give a tithe to the Levites (members of the tribe of Levi not of Aaronide descent — who assisted the Kohanim in the discharge of their functions). Since the Kohanim and the Levites had no land possessions, they were free of the tasks of laboring and tending the soil. Their livelihoods were to be provided by the entire people of Israel. What was the task of the sons of Levi to be? They were to teach God's judgments to Jacob and His Torah to Israel. Some of them presided over courts of law throughout the land. Others rendered judgement in matters of ritual law. From them came judges, scribes, teachers for children, in all of Israel's dwelling places, in city and village.

A VOLUNTARY GIFT

It might be asked: "Since the livelihood of the Levites was to be dependent on offerings and tithes, would it not have been proper to collect the latter by compulsory means rather than by voluntary ones, which might prove unreliable? Was it wise to allow the owners of the fields to gather their produce into storehouses or into their homes prior to the collection of tithes?"

The response to such a question could thus be stated: It was the precise intention of the Torah, that a person should set aside his offerings and tithes alone, and of his free will, in the privacy of his storehouse or home; at a time when no policemen or guards would see him, other than God alone.

The commandment to give offerings and tithes was not given for the advantage of the prospective recipients but rather of the givers of such offerings. It was intended as a reminder to every Jewish person that it was the Lord his God who had given him his inheritance; as a reminder of his obligation to fulfill what God required of him; as a reminder of the purpose for which he had been given his inheritance, and for which God had chosen him from amongst all the peoples. Therefore, each individual was bidden to set aside his tithes from his storehouse and his wine cellar with his own hands, or through a messenger appointed by him voluntarily. Through such an act of Hafrasha (setting aside), a Jewish person declares to his God: "My land inheritance — is Yours, the fruit it brings forth — are Yours. You gave us this precious land so that we might eat of its fruit and be satiated with its goodness, because of Your love of Israel and Your compassion for Your people; I set aside what You commanded, first. By Your permission do I eat what remains — 'Blessed art Thou, O Lord, our God, King of the universe, who sanctified us with His commandments and commanded us to set aside offerings and tithes.'"

The land is entirely holy to God. All that grows on it is sacred. And we are not permitted to derive benefits from its produce without the word of the King of the universe. Whoever derives such benefit without permission, is as if he had desecrated the holy. The King states: "Do as I bid and you will be granted permission to eat of what is holy to Me; set aside Terumah (an offering) from the fruit of the land and the Terumah will be permitted to the Kohanim who serve Me; the remainder of the produce will then be permitted for all others. After both Kohanim and Israelites give thanks to Him who gave them dominion over the fruit of their land, they may eat and be satisfied. Both the Kohen, who eats the Terumah, and the Israelite, who eats of the Chullin (unsanctified produce), receive their gift from the Divine table. From the hand of God and by His commandment, do they receive their portions. But if they fail to do the King's bidding and do not set apart Terumah from Chullin, then the produce of their land remains consecrated. Who permitted them derivation of benefit from Hekdesh (anything consecrated)? Therefore, produce from which Terumah has not yet been set apart, is prohibited both to the Kohen and to the Israelite.

We are taught then: until the act of "setting apart," the entire yield of the field is consecrated. After the "setting apart," the Terumah remains partly consecrated, and may be eaten only by Kohanim. Until one has fulfilled God's will by setting apart the prescribed offerings, he is not yet deserving that what is consecrated to God should become Chullin and permitted to him. After his fulfillment of his Creator's commandment, he becomes deserving of deriving "profane" benefit from what had previously been consecrated to God. In the giving of Terumah and Maaser (tithes), the act of "setting apart" is therefore seen to be the most significant part of the mitzvah.

Therefore, the Rabbis prescribed the utterance of the blessing over the "setting apart" rather than over the presentation of the offering. If a person places a basket containing all his fruit into the hands of the Kohen, he has not fulfilled the commandment until the Terumah has been set apart from the remaining fruit, by the Kohen. Till then the entire basket is forbidden both to him and to the Kohen. The essential part of the mitzvah has not yet been performed, and the produce is consecrated to God alone. The Israelite cannot give what is not yet his and the Kohen cannot receive an object which does not yet belong to the one who gives it. But if the Kohen has set apart Terumah from the produce, the royal commandment has been performed, and the entire produce belongs to the Kohen. What was lacking before? The act of giving was not lacking. It was the "setting apart" which was lacking, and which alone renders the produce permitted for benefit.

Nor should we wonder over this. For most of the mitzvoth of the Torah are dependent on the principle of separation. God has rendered man's deeds and his speech capable of achieving distinction between the various degrees of the holy, between the sacred and the profane, between light and darkness, between Israel and the nations, and between the seventh day and the six work days of the week. (For, if a person makes of all the seven days of the week a continuous Sabbath day and does not distinguish between them, he does not achieve the experience of the holiness of the Sabbath at all.)

Say then: the essential aspect of the commandments addressed to the people of Israel in the matter of Offerings and Tithes, is not that of the payment of a tax from their belongings, but is rather the act of "setting apart," so that they may know thereby that all the Earth and its blessings is of God. He created it and gives it to whomever He finds suitable. By His will He gives it to this one, and by His will He takes it from the first and gives it to another. Since therefore, "separation" is the essence of the mitzvah, it is fulfilled only voluntarily and through conscious intention. For, where there is no freedom of intention and no knowledge (of the character of the act), there is no "separation" and distinction.

THE LEVITES ARE TO ENTER YOUR HOME FREELY

A person ought not to say: "Since the Offerings and Tithes belong not to me but to the Kohanim and the Levites, I ought not to distribute them to a particular Kohen or Levite of my choice.

It would be better for me to bring all my Tithes to some place commonly owned by the Kohanim, or to deliver them to the possession of the court; wherefrom the Kohanim might divide the gathered offerings among themselves."

Such is not the most excellent manner by which the mitzvah is performed. The mitzvah is performed at best, when the Kohen or Levite comes to the storehouse and takes his tithes therefrom, upon the owner's desire that the gift be his. And the owner of the field is permitted to say: "To such and such a Kohen do I give my Terumah, to such and such a Levite do I give my Maaser."

Why is this so? For, as we have said earlier, these gifts are intended for the good of their givers rather than for the good of their recipients. It would be easier for the Levites if their gifts were brought to their homes. It would be still easier that they be given inheritances, as all Israel is, so that they might not need their brothers' gifts.

The Lord however commanded, for the sake of Israel's holiness, that some acquire inheritances and labor their lands, while others are bidden to engage in the study of Torah — and eat, with their brothers, of the fruit of the land which God has given them. The striving of each is different from that of the other. They remain however, equal in holiness and glory. We may derive this knowledge from the fact that their table is one, and they eat from one field and one storehouse.

The same is also true concerning the actual giving (of Terumah and Maaser). Better that the Levite should come to the home of the farmer, rather than that the latter should bring his gifts to the Levite's home, leave them there, and return to his home. For just as their table is one, their Torah is to be one. When the Levite enters the storehouse of the Israelite, he gets to know the latter and his family. He becomes close to them and becomes aware of their needs. He teaches them Torah, and imparts knowledge to them. He guides their sons and daughters in the way of the Law; and thereby imbues Israel's homes with knowledge of Torah and love of mitzvoth.

YOUR FIRST DOUGH — CHALLAH

Not only the produce of the grain storehouse and wine cellar are subject to the "setting apart" of Terumah. Even if one has already set apart his Terumah and Maaser, has brought his flour

121

home and kneaded dough to bake his bread — he is commanded by the Torah to again "set apart" an offering for the Kohen — Terumah from the dough. The Kohen will thus see him and his ways at home, and will be able to cast the spirit of holiness upon his home. The people and the Kohen are to have one Torah, one field, and one table. For together, they are a kingdom of Kohanim and a holy people.

THE TITHE FOR THE POOR

During two years of every seven year cycle (the third and the sixth years), a person is obligated to "set apart" from the fruit of his soil a tithe for the poor, the stranger, the orphan, and the widow; in addition to the Terumah and Maaser which he "sets apart" for the Kohen and the Levite respectively. As is the case with Terumah and Maaser Rishon (the first tithe — which goes to the Levite), if one fails to formally "set apart" Maaser Ani (the tithe for the poor) the entire basket is prohibited for use even if Terumah and Maaser Rishon have already been "set apart."

For "the poor will never cease from the midst of the land." Sometimes it happens that a person is forced to sell his parental inheritance; in whch instance his land will not return to him till the Jubilee year (every fiftieth year was designated the Jubilee year, and all land sold during the previous fifty years had to be returned to the original owners). Or, there might be a Ger Toshav (a "resident-stranger" — one who had embraced the seven Noahide laws and could thus acquire the rights and privileges of residence in the land of Israel) whose ancestors had not acquired a portion in the land at the time of the distribution of the land to the tribes of Israel, and who therefore had no land of his own. Or, there might be orphans or widows incapable of tending their inheritance and rendering it fruitful.

"Take care," the Torah therefore says to the Jew, "lest you forget the stranger, the orphan, the widow or the poor. When you eat of the bread of the land, know that the land and its fullness belongs to the Lord alone. The food which He prepared for His creatures, He prepared for them all. If food for a poor person is not available in his home, it is available in your home. The food he needs, is his, not yours. And when you give him his Maaser, it is not charity which you give him. Rather are your returning what belongs to him. When you make the return, do so graciously, as one does who returns an object temporarily entrusted to him for safekeeping.

Therefore, the essence of this mitzvah too is the act of "setting apart." By the charge of your King and the bidding of Him who nourishes and sustains you in His goodness, you are obligated to "set aside" the portion of the poor, and to place it at the side of the basket. Then, God will shine His countenance upon you also, and He will give you the remainder of the fruit.

The Kohen acquires his portion first. After him comes the Levite. The poor, the stranger, the orphan and the widow come next. And you — come last.

If you have already "set apart" the required Terumah and Maaser offerings, you too may eat your bread in joy, for God has graciously acknowledged your deeds. Even if you have not yet actually given the offerings already "set apart," to their respective recipients, the remainder of your produce is already permitted to you. When you "set apart" your Terumah and Maaser offerings you thereby achieved the right to enjoy the remnant of your produce. For, in the act of "setting apart," you acknowledged God's ownership of the land, His being the source of your bounty, and the consequent claim of others to their rightful portion of your bounty. Likewise, does God grant you your portion and He says: "What remains -- is for you. Let it be yours!" At the same time, there is perfect certainty that whoever "sets apart" a portion for others from his possessions, will hand it over to its intended recipients. For, who ever keeps the portion of the poor in his possession, and fails to give it to them, is not withholding charity, but is rather in possession of stolen property. And the people of Israel are not given to such malicious wrongdoing.

THE TORAH IS THE POSSESSION OF ALL ISRAEL

God wanted to grant Israel the merit of Torah and mitzvoth. He therefore allotted to the rich the task of sustaining the poor. Similarly, did He entrust to those who are engaged in worldly pursuits the sustenance of the students of the Torah, so that both might achieve the merit of this world and the next one.

The Torah of one who labors the soil is not firmly rooted in his life. When however, he associates with the Levite and makes the Levite welcome in his home, the latter becomes his teacher and guide. And the man of the soil is thereby saved from rebellion against God, from boorishness and from forgetfulness of the Torah and of Him who gave it. However, he will still not find sufficient time or strength left after his daily labors, to draw nourishment from the well-springs of Torah till his soul be satisfied by its waters. Can it be that God has given the Torah only to the Levites, to an elect few whose time is free? Was the Torah given for them alone to enjoy its goodness and plumb its depths?

God therefore gave to the entire people of Israel a number of commandments whose purpose was the provision of freedom, for those who observe them, from the burdens of daily labor at periodic intervals. The free time thus acquired, could be dedicated to the study of Torah and the worship of God. These commandments were designed to make of farmers, scholars of the Torah; they were intended to transform tillers of the soil into Sages capable of probing the mysteries of wisdom; till, as it were, their studies might become their essential vocation, and their other labors secondary ones.

The mitzvoth here referred to are: the Sabbath and holidays for rest from daily work; the cessation of work in the fields during the Shemittah and Jubilee years to give rest to the soil; and several other tithes (to be explained later) which required "ascent to Jerusalem" periodically, with time set aside during those visits for the study of Torah and the acquisition of wisdom.

One day every week, the Sabbath day, every Jewish person was to be free from all labor. That day was to be consecrated to God, to the study of Torah, to prayer, to the rejoicing of the soul and the enlargement of knowledge, to the acquisition of wisdom and the serenity of the heart.

Seven days every year were prescribed as festival days by the Torah (the remaining festival days were prescribed by Rabbinic decree). Those days were consecrated to the pursuit of freedom for the soul, to the purification and refinement of the soul, to the rejoicing and expansion of the heart.

One of every seven years, eight years in every fifty year Jubilee period, the farmer was to forsake the plough, the scythe, and all his other farming implements. He was to give rest to his field and his vineyard that entire year. The Torah assured him that God would cast blessing upon his land and would cause his produce during the sixth year to be sufficient till the time of reaping in the eighth year. The land was "to rest a Sabbath to the Lord," and those who labored on it were also "to rest a Sabbath to the Lord" their God. What are people to do with so long a period of rest; with sustenance for the given period provided for them by God; whose land is blessed, whose heart is filled with thanksgiving and trust, and whose soul yearns for truth and knowledge? No days were as pleasant to Israel as those. For during those days every Jewish person reviewed and restudied all that he knew of the Torah, and acquired a new "portion" of its wisdom, which he then could teach to his children. The people of Israel were similar in those days to their forefathers who had eaten Manna from heaven in their time. Their food was bread from the heavens, and they studied the Torah of the land.

YOU SHALL RISE AND ASCEND

The Torah is beloved by the people of Israel and is studied by it in all places and in all times. In Jerusalem, throughout the land of Israel, in all the lands of Israel's dwelling — not a single place is devoid of the study of Torah. Especially fervent however, is Israel's love of the study of Torah in the place in which God chose to cause His name to dwell — in Jerusalem; towards which the eyes of all Israel are lifted. Most of Israel's great men, her elders, sages and judges, the great Sanhedrin, are in Jerusalem. In Jerusalem the study of Torah and performance of mitzvoth are intensely pursued. Whoever comes to Jerusalem comes to the palace of the Torah. And if one comes to the palace of the Torah, he cannot but be refined thereby. Jerusalem — in which the sanctuary stands — is similar to a shop filled with fragrant spices — whoever enters becomes fragrant himself; to a well of living waters — whoever drinks of its waters is refreshed.

Therefore, God gave Israel the pilgrim festivals — "Three times during the year all your males shall appear before the Lord, the God of hosts." "And they shall not appear before Me empty handed." Any offerings which you have pledged at home, you are to bring with you in order to present them to God. Every tenth one of the cattle and sheep born to you this year is consecrated to God, and when you go up to Jerusalem you are to take your animal tithes with you for a peace offering on the Altar. The meat therefrom is to be consumed by the owners in purity of body, in rejoicing of the soul and in thanksgiving, within the sanctified walls of Jerusalem. The Levite, the stranger, the orphan and the widow are to join the owners at table, all together are to

125

rest in the shadow of the wings of the Divine Presence and dwell on God's Torah in unison.

No year may pass, without the "setting apart" of two tithes from one's fruit, in addition to the offering presented to the Kohen. The Terumah offering to the Kohen and the "first tithe" to the Levite are constant. There remains one other tithe whose character varies. Every third and sixth of the Shemittah years, the second tithe is designated for the poor and is thus called: "The tithe of the poor." During the remaining Shemittah years, the first, second, fourth and fifth — it is designated simply, the second tithe.

What is the character of this tithe?

Its owners are not obligated to give it to others. They themselves bring it up to Jerusalem, or redeem it for an equivalent money value, which they bring to Jerusalem and for which they purchase food, to be consumed by them in purity and rejoicing during the entire period of their stay in Jerusalem.

Similarly — if a person plants a vineyard or a garden or any fruit growing tree, or if he grafts onto his trees branches of the same kind in order to improve them, all their fruit shall be forbidden for use or benefit during the first three years. Their fourth yield of fruit is to be brought by their owner to Jerusalem, where he is to enjoy them in a state of purity in rejoicing and song, in praise and thanksgiving to God.

For what purpose is all this to be done? In order that a person going up to Jerusalem to pursue the study of Torah, may have his food readily available; that his time may be free and his heart open to absorb teachings of Torah from the mouths of the elders of the people and the Sanhedrin, the scholars and sages who dwell in Jerusalem. For, Torah studied in any other place is not as the Torah studied in Jerusalem. Torah studied in distraction is not as Torah studied in a state of relaxation. And a person does not achieve relaxation of mind other than through rejoicing. And there is no place in which a state of rejoicing prevailed as constantly as in Jerusalem.

Come and see how beloved are the mitzvoth of "setting aside" Terumah and Maaser. For, concerning all the commandments of the Torah, a person may not test God and say: "I will fulfill the commandments and see what reward God will give me!" And whoever tests God violates a prohibition of the Torah, for it is said: "You shall not test the Lord your God" (Deut. 6). These mitzvoth (of Terumah and Maaser) are different, however. Concerning them, a person is permitted to put God to the test and to say: "I offer a tithe from my fruit in accordance with your commandment, and I wish to see what blessing you will give me." For thus does the Prophet say: "Bring all the tithes, etc., and test me with this, said the Lord God, if I will not open unto you the windows of the heavens and will cast blessing upon you without end."

WHEN THE SANCTUARY STOOD

When the Sanctuary stood, every Jewish person was able to fulfill these commandments to perfection.

The act of setting aside was one commandment and the act of giving was another. The "setting aside" — was done privately. For the act of giving, there was testimony — that of the recipients. But this testimony in itself was not deemed sufficient. Once in three years, every Jewish person went up to Jerusalem, to the courtyard of the house of the Lord, and there he testified concerning himself, before God: "I have put away the hallowed things out of my house, and also have given them unto the Levite, and unto the stranger, to the orphan, and to the widow, according to all Thy commandments, which Thou hast commanded me; I have not transgressed any of Thy commandments, neither have I forgotten them. I have not eaten thereof in my mourning, neither have I put away thereof, being unclean, nor given thereof for the dead; I have hearkened to the voice of the Lord my God; I have done according to all that Thou hast commanded me. Look forth from Thy holy habitation, from heaven, and bless Thy people Israel, and the land which Thou hast given us, as Thou didst swear unto our fathers, a land flowing with milk and honey" (Deut. 26) Greater was this testimony which a Jewish person uttered concerning himself in the place of the sanctuary, than any other testimony in the world. For, he then stood and bore witness in the presence of the King of Kings, the Holy One, Blessed Be He, Who probes the depths of the heart.

Still another testimony was uttered by every Jewish person in the place in which God chose to rest His name — a testimony that he was not ungrateful, that he was not filled with pride, that he had not forgotten his lowly beginnings, that he remembered God's kindnesses unto him. This second testimony was uttered at the time of the bringing of one's first fruit (Bikkurim). Thus do we read in the Mishnah (Tractate Bikurim, Chapter 3):

"How were the Bikkurim set aside? A man goes down into his field, he sees a fig that ripened, or a cluster of grapes that ripened, or a pomegranate that ripened, he ties a red rope around it and says: "Let these be Bikkurim.""

"How were the Bikkurim taken up (to Jerusalem)? All (the inhabitants of) the cities that constituted the Maamad (the name of a group of Israelite representatives who discharged specific religious tasks for their communities) assembled in the city of the Maamad (where the leader resided), and spent the night in the open place thereof without entering any of the houses. Early in the morning the officer said: 'Let us arise and go up to Zion, into the house of the Lord our God.'

"Those who lived near brought fresh figs and grapes, but those from a distance brought dried figs and raisins. An ox with horns bedecked with gold and with an olive crown on his head led the way. The flute was played before them until they were near Jerusalem; and when they arrived close to Jerusalem they sent messengers in advance (to advise the residents of Jerusalem of their coming), and ornamentally arrayed their Bikkurim. The governors and chiefs and treasurers (of the Temple) went out to meet them. According to the rank of the entrants used they to go forth. All the skilled artisans of Jerusalem would stand up before them and greet them: 'Brethren, men of such and such a place, we are delighted to welcome you.'

"The flute was playing before them till they reached the Temple mount; and when they reached the Temple mount even King Agrippa would take the basket and place it on his shoulder and walk as far as the Temple court. At the approach to the court, the Levites would sing the song: 'I will extol Thee o Lord, for Thou hast raised me up, and hast not suffered mine enemies to rejoice over me.'

"While the basket was yet on his shoulder he would recite: 'I profess this day unto the Lord my God that I have come into the land which the Lord swore to our fathers to give it to us (and I am not ungrateful) etc. A wandering Aramean was my father (Jacob, who had no possession in his land), he went down to Egypt and sojourned there (as a stranger and not as a resident). He became there a great and mighty people (it is Your great kindness to us, o Lord, that You did not allow us to be destroyed in Egypt). And the Egyptians harmed us and they afflicted us, and they put upon us rigorous labor and we cried out to the Lord, the

God of our fathers (our hand did not help us but —) the Lord heard our voice — and the Lord delivered us from Egypt with a strong hand — and He brought us to this place and gave us this land which flows with milk and honey. Now I have brought the first fruit of the land which Thou hast given me, o Lord.'" He would then complete the entire passage. Finally, he would deposit the basket by the side of the altar, prostrate himself and depart.

THE SETTING APART OF OFFERINGS AND TITHES TODAY

Thus were these mitzvoth performed when the Sanctuary stood. Now that the Sanctuary is in ruins, because of our sins, and the laws of ritual purity are no longer adhered to, and we have neither Kohen nor Levite to perform the Temple rites, the act of giving Terumah and Maaser is lost to us. For if we were to give to the Kohen any of the offerings prescribed for him, he could not eat them, since he is unable nowadays to purify himself of the state of ritual defilement which is common to us all. And Terumah or any hallowed object may be eaten only in a state of ritual purity (Taharah).

Shall we also forsake the mitzvah of "setting apart" Terumah and Maaser, because we no longer are able to perform the mitzvah of giving Terumah and Maaser to their respective recipients? But the mitzvah of "setting apart" is not dependent on the act of giving. Each is a separate commandment. When we perform the act of giving our offerings to those who properly receive them, we do so for our benefit and pleasure. We wish thereby to extend to others the blessing which is ours. Because of our sins, that pleasure was taken from us. The Sanctuary is still in ruins. But when we "set apart" Terumah and Maaser from our produce, or when we "set apart" Challah from the dough, we do so not for benefit or pleasure but as an act of testimony and a sign of faith.

For the "setting apart" of Challah, Terumah and Maaser is a testimony by the people of Israel, that the deeds of our hands, the fruit of our labor, the yield of our fields, are all given to us from the hand of God. It is testimony on our part, that the Earth and its fullness belong to God, that all our striving is consecrated to God. We also testify thereby, that we accept upon ourselves God's decrees and that we do not derive benefit from anything hallowed, till we fulfill His commandments and set aside what He com-

129

manded us to. And only then do we eat of what remains. This testimony we do not forsake even in our days.

Precisely because we have lost the ability to perform the mitzvah of giving Terumah and Maaser presently, we are all the more obligated to strengthen this faith in ourselves; so that we might thereby correct what we have "blemished" in earlier generations. In earlier generations blessing rested constantly on the land of milk and honey. All the same, our forefathers sinned and failed to give thanks for the blessing of the land. They nullified God's commandments concerning the land. And now — though the fullness of blessing does not yet rest on our land, all the same we are capable of giving thanks to God and uttering blessing to Him for the goodness of the land. Beloved is our land to us for having remained loyal to us even in desolation; for not having given its strength to the nations who conquered it; for having waited for us and for continuing to wait for us. We are not ungrateful for this land of ours though its desolation is not yet removed. Every fruit it produces is beloved to us and sacred to us. We do not desecrate its holiness by eating its fruit before "setting aside" its required offerings. First we set aside what we are reqired to, and only thereafter do we eat of the remainder.

There is indeed an aspect of importance in the act of setting apart Terumah and Maaser nowadays which was lacking when the Sanctuary still stood. For in our time the act of "setting apart" is entirely for the sake of heaven and we derive no benefit or pleasure from it. No one derives pleasure from it, and no one utters thanks to those who perform it. The only reason for the performance of the mitzvah today, is the fulfillment of God's decree unto us, and the intention to thereby purify our lives, so that we might deserve to see the erection of the Sanctuary in our day again; and so that we might then be able to perform the mitzvah in its entirety.

We see then that the mitzvah of "setting apart" Terumah and Maaser applies in the land of Israel even today, and observant Jews loyally abide by its requirements and do not forsake it.

THE "SETTING APART" OF CHALLAH — A PARAMOUNT MITZVAH

We have stated thus far that the mitzvah of setting apart Terumah and Maaser is binding and of great importance even at the present time. However the commandment to set apart Challah from the dough or from the dough already baked, is of even greater importance. For it also applies outside the land of Israel, by Rabbinic decree. Why did the Rabbis prescribe the setting apart of Challah outside the land? So that the law of Challah might not be forgotten by Israel. For the mitzvah of Challah is entrusted to every Jewish man and woman, whether he or she have a field or not. And there is no Jewish home in which the opportunity does not occur to perform this mitzvah many a time during the entire year. The time will come when the communities of the Diaspora will be ingathered to the land of Israel, and the entire people of Israel will dwell in their own land. They may say: "Yesterday we did not set apart Challah from our dough — we shall not do so today either!' and the law of Challah might be forgotten by Israel, Heaven forbid. Therefore the Sages prescribed that the mitzvah of Challah should be obligatory at all times, and wherever Jews dwell; so that their attachment to it might never be weakened.

Whoever fulfills the mitzvah of setting apart Challah is doubly rewarded by God. For he abides by the prescription of the Torah: 'You shall not turn aside from the thing they tell you (the Rabbis), to the right or to the left' (Deut. 17). In addition, one who performs this mitzvah thereby indicates that he eagerly awaits the redemption of Israel which is soon to come; and he therefore habituates himself to the performance of mitzvoth in anticipation of the return of Israel to the land of Israel, when those mitzvoth will again become obligatory. Whoever yearns for the redemption of Israel merits the sight of the consolation of Israel. Let us then abide by these mitzvoth and not forsake them, and as reward, we will merit the experience of the final redemption of Israel and the building of God's chosen house speedily in our days, Amen.

THE SETTING APART OF CHALLAH

1. *There are five types of grain which, if one made flour from them and prepared a dough, are subject to the mitzvah to set apart Challah. They are: Wheat, barley, spelt, rye, and oats.*

2. *He who sets apart Challah recites the blessing: "Blessed art Thou o Lord our God, King of the Universe, who has sanctified us with His commandments and has commanded us to set apart Challah." After the benediction, he sets apart a Kazayith (literally the equivalent sive of an olive) from the dough and says: "this is to be Challah." He is to burn it immediately or to leave it in a place where people will not eat it by error.*

3. *A dough is not subject to the mitzvah of Challah unless it meets the following three conditions: it contains 1680 grams (3.69 lbs.) of flour, it is kneaded with water, and is to be bake. entirely or in part in an oven or on a dry pan. If the dough contains more than 1248 grams (2.74 lbs.) of flour but less than 1680 grams, or if it is kneaded with eggs, oil, or fruit juices or if it is to be entirely cooked in a pot or fried in oil — then if the dough is thick, Challah is to be set apart from it, but a benediction is not to be uttered. But, if the dough contains less than 1248 grams of flour — the mitzvah of Challah does not apply to it at all.*

4. *Dough that is dried out or broken into pieces, is not subject to Challah.*

5. *If a person mixed flour from the above mentioned five species of grain and made one dough, the dough is subject to Challah. But if he kneaded each species separately and then attached the doughs to each other, they are not joined together for the required measurement of Challah other than in the following manner: A wheat dough is joined only with a spelt dough. A barley dough is joined with any*

of the species with the exception of wheat. A spelt dough is joined with any of the other species. An oats dough is joined with a dough made of barley or spelt. Similarly, a rye dough is joined with barley and spelt alone. All other combinations of two doughs, even if they be completely attached to each other, are not subject to Challah unless there is sufficient quantity in each dough to render it subject sidered as two doughs, and are not subject to the mitzvah

6. *The doughs are considered as joined to one another (for the measure of Challah), only if they are attached to each other in such a manner that each cannot be separated from the other without tearing away part of the other. But if they are completely separable from each other and neither draws along any of the dough of the other they are con- to the mitzvah.*
of Challah, unless each one has the necessary quantity of dough by itself.

7. *If one kneads small doughs and puts them into an oven (into one enclosure with surrounding walls) and in the oven they became attached to each other or even if they were baked separately but were subsequently put together into one utensil which covers all the bakeries together — then they are all "added to each other" in determining the size of the dough, and Challah is to be set apart therefrom after the baking.*

8. *If one kneads two doughs or more, which are of one species and are each subject to Challah, he may set apart Challah from any one of them for the remainder; but only if all the doughs are placed near one another.*

9. *If a dough was subject to the mitzvah of Challah before baking, but its owners forgot to set apart its Challah, they do so after the baking and utter the required benediction.*

10. *It is not permissible to set apart Challah on the Sabbath. On a holiday it is permissible to set apart Challah only from a dough kneaded the same day.*

11. *If one forgot to set apart Challah on Erev Shabbat (Friday) or on Erev Yom Tov (the day preceding a holiday), in the land of Israel — anything baked from the dough may not be eaten till after the Sabbath or the holiday.*

Outside the land of Israel — one may eat such bakeries, but he is to leave a part uneaten from which to set apart Challah after the Sabbath or the holiday. It is however forbidden, in such an instance to leave only the part of the dough which he intends to use as Challah. Rather must he leave more dough than he will need for Challah itself, so that some should remain for eating after the Challah has been set apart.

12.   *The mitzvah of setting apart Challah is obligatory upon men and women. But it is the custom of the daughters of Israel to seek to perform the mitzvah themselves, since they are the foundation of the Jewish home.*

CHAPTER 20

THE SANCTIFIED TABLE (KASHRUTH)

The Holy One, Blessed be He, was desirous of granting merit to Israel; He therefore gave them an abundance of Torah and of observances — observances intended to accompany man on all his ways, and in all his deeds. Thus is it written: "In all thy ways, acknowledge Him" (Proverbs 3). The observances which accompany the Jew constantly, are a crown upon his head; and they exalt him above the remainder of creation. One who does his work in the field, who builds for himself a house in which to dwell, who makes for himself garments to wear, who pursues the various activities of life, but acts in all of them in accordance with his own view or intention — is not similar to one who is motivated in all those self-same deeds by the intention and the command of his Maker. It is the Sovereign of the universe Who commands him: Do thus! Refrain from doing thus!

One who acts purely on the basis of his own understanding walks alone in his world; his path is not secure, he is in constant fear of stumbling and falling. But one whose actions are dictated by the wisdom of his Maker — how good is his portion, how pleasant his lot! For, can a man know greater glory, or possess a more beautiful crown than the knowledge that God Himself leads him to safety, saves him from the pit and the snare, and guards him from fear and worry. With God does he walk in his world. The Lord is his light and his salvation — whom shall he fear?

Just as the Holy One, Blessed be He, crowned the deeds of Man, and gave him observances to keep, while he labors in the field, when he is at home, as he walks on the way — thus also did He crown the Jewish table by sanctifying with His commandments the food eaten at that table. You will find that, of the 613 commandments which God gave to Israel, at least 50 are to be observed at table. Eating is the first human instinct. It accompanies man throughout life, from the moment of birth to the last day on earth. And it is to this instinct that the Torah addresses itself, disciplining, purifying, sublimating it. The instinct says: Eat, drink, and rejoice, for tomorrow we die. But the Torah says: First make sure that the food you wish to eat is not prohibited; that it has been correctly slaughtered; that the animal's death has not been such as to render it *trefa*. Be sure to wait the proper interval between eating meat and dairy foods; wait until you have recited the proper blessing. On Sabbaths and holy days first utter the blessing sanctifying that day; wait until the fast day is over before eating. Your motto should be not "Eat, drink, and rejoice, for tomorrow we die" — but "Eat, drink, and rejoice, obeying God's commandments — and live!"

WHY KASHRUTH?

The Jewish people is a people sanctified; we do not question the decrees of God, either before or after we obey them. We do not keep asking why God has prohibited one food and permitted another. For us it is sufficient that such is the will of the Sovereign of the universe. God's will, for us, is the sole and final determinant, whether the reasons be explicit or not.

In fact, we bless and praise God for *not* having made the reasons for these observances more explicit. Had He done so, we might have been inclined not to obey, or we might perform his commandments for the sake of our own relative convenience, rather than for His absolute love and awe. We should be serving ourselves, not our Maker.

Then, there would always be the possibility, were the reasons for these observances explicit, that scholars would argue: "The particular reason that the Torah gives for obeying this particular commandment has significance only in a given time or place. In our time and place that reason has lost its significance — one need no longer obey." As it is, we know that unless otherwise clearly stated, the observances the Creator has decreed apply to all times and all places.

Yet we know, as a general rule, the purpose of all the observances. God being good, His decrees are all intended for the good of His creatures. We were given them for our own happiness and pleasure. In the words of King David: "O consider and see that the Lord is good" (Psalms 34).

He who created the universe and established the laws of nature expresses His will in nature. Certainly, it was His desire that His creatures should not drown in the sea, nor enter fire and be burned; all the same He did not warn us in advance to avoid being drowned or burned to death. Rather, he so fixed the nature of water and fire that they protect themselves from intrusion and death. Similarly, He could have so made man that he would be incapable of eating those foods that are forbidden him by God; or He might have made those foods beneficent to man, and therefore permitted. But instead He gave man freedom of choice — in order to purify and ennoble him. He who refrains from a wrong act not because he has no desire to perform it but because an iron curtain stands between him and the performance of that deed — because it is against his nature — is far less to be praised than he who is "fenced in by roses" — the roses of God's commandments. It would be easy to tread those roses under foot, for they are fragile. But, cherishing the beauty and fragrance of God's roses, we practice self-control and stay inside the fence. In exerting this self-control, we are purified and refined.

FROM OUR SAGES' COMMENTS ON KASHRUTH

Our sages have commented: "Scripture reads: 'For I have set you apart from the peoples, that ye should be Mine.' The meaning is: When you are apart from the other peoples of the earth, then you are Mine; if not, you belong to Nebuchadnezzar, king of Babylon, and his ilk." (Sifra Kedoshim).

We are set apart from the peoples of the earth by our acceptance of God's separation of us through His commandments, not by the assumption that we accept these commandments because they fit our own pleasures and conveniences, and would have done so even if the Torah had not commanded them.

In the words of our sages: "Said Rabbi Eliezer the son of Azariah: 'A man ought not to say: I do not wish to eat of the flesh of pig, I do not wish immoral intercourse. Rather he should say: I do wish to do these things, but how can I, since my Father in heaven has decreed otherwise.' We know this because it is written in Scripture: 'For I have set you apart from the peoples, that ye should be Mine.' That is the reason why we forsake wrong doing and accept the yoke of the kingdom of heaven." (Sifra ibid.)

Our sages have made this quite clear: "The commandments were given us only for the purification and ennobling of God's creatures." This is true even of those commandments whose reason we know — such as the prohibition against the marriage of close relatives, and the eating of worms and insects. We Jews observe them primarily because they are a Divine decree. There is no better reason.

ONE TABLE FOR ALL ISRAEL.

The Torah speaks of the distinctiveness of Israel, as reflected in the many practices that set us apart from other peoples. The difference between our table and theirs is one of the greatest importance. Throughout the generations our people have been so convinced of the importance of kashruth that even the poorest and hungriest have disdained the most lavish meals where the food was not kosher. Shall we now allow separation between Jewish parents and children, between brothers and brothers, at our tables by some of us not practicing kashruth while others do?

Scripture says: "For I am the Lord that brought you up out of the land of Egypt, to be your God; ye shall therefore be holy, for I am holy." (Leviticus 11.) On this the sages commented: "God said, 'I brought you up out of the land of Egypt only on condition that you accept the yoke of My commandments. For whosoever acknowledges that yoke also acknowledges the exodus from Egypt, and whosoever rejects that yoke, rejects the exodus from Egypt. 'To be your God' — whether you consent or not. 'For I am holy' — as I am holy and separate, so shall you be holy and separate.' " (Sifra Shemini 110.)

Liberation from the oppression of other peoples and rejection of the yoke of God's commandments are two ends of the same rope. No one can hold both ends at the same time; it is one or the other. The Jew who rejects the yoke of God's commandments erects a barrier between himself and his Jewish brethren. He tries to lose the outward mark of his Jewish identity, denying, so to speak, that his ancestors ever really left Egypt to become a Chosen People, one destined to live apart. But we have been chosen, willy-nilly, by the act of Exodus. We are separated from the peoples of the earth by our destiny.

The Jewish people as a community cannot separate themselves from God, however great their transgression. For the Holy One, blessed be He, will never repudiate His covenant with us — and we certainly cannot. In the words of Scripture: "As the mountains are round about Jerusalem, so the Lord is round about His people from this time and for ever" (Psalms 125). "Ye are the children of the Lord your God" (Deuteronomy 14). We are surrounded by God, we cannot escape Him. We are God's children, and can never be divorced from our Father in Heaven. Though we sin, He is patient: He metes out punishment, then renews His covenant.

But our imitation of other peoples, though it be meant as flattery, never has led them to love us the more. Their hatred of us is complex and deep-rooted, rooted in the historic destiny of the human race. We cannot rely on their mercy, and we must not separate from our tradition in a vain attempt to win their favor through our disunity.

The Torah, in warning us against eating forbidden foods, implies three dire consequences: "Neither shall ye make yourselves unclean with them, that ye should be defiled thereby" (Leviticus 11). Forbidden foods defile those that consume them. They cause us to lose the capacity to distinguish between good and evil. And, in the end, they lead to the loss of Jewish identity.

KASHRUTH AS NECESSARY FOR JEWISH EXISTENCE

Different beings require different circumstances in order to live. The same is true of peoples.

Some will advance the argument: Why deprive ourselves of so many foods eaten by other peoples, of the pleasures the majority derives? Why limit ourselves unnecessarily? Other peoples flourish on the same foods the Torah prohibits to us."

But we are not like other peoples, and our life is not theirs. They cannot live according to the Torah's decrees. But Israel cannot survive a single hour without them. For they are, literally, "our life and the length of our days." Without them, we should die as a people.

THE "REMNANTS OF THE ALTAR"

Our tradition relates that the flesh of the animals listed in the story of Noah, that he brough as sacrificial offerings, was afterward designated as permitted. The righteous Gentiles also partook of that flesh in Noah's time; the patriarchs, in turn, restricted themselves to the flesh known as the "remnants of an offering brought on an altar."

The Torah uses the same phrase, telling us that so long as our forefathers dwelled in the wilderness on their way to the land of Canaan, they could eat only flesh that was "the remnant of an altar." Eventually, when the children of Israel settled in their own land, they were permitted to eat food of animals that had been slaughtered according to the designated rules.

When Israel received the Torah, all those animals which had previously been designated as unclean were specifically forbidden them. In general, these are the predatory, wild animals. The prohibition against consuming blood aims at preventing the brutalization of the person who consumes it.

In general, we may say of kashruth: God alone knows the secrets of life. He alone knows the ultimate end of all things. We can do no better than to rely on Him, and on His promise that our well-being, our very life itself, depend on a scrupulous observance of the laws of kashruth.

CONCERNING THE PROHIBITION OF BLOOD

1. *Only the blood of animals, beasts and fowl is forbidden. The blood of fish and locusts is permitted.*

2. *Blood absorbed into the flesh of animals, beasts and fowl, which does not flow out of the flesh is permitted, but if the blood can flow out of the flesh, then it is forbidden.*

3. *For this reason one may not cook meat unless one first removes all the blood which is likely to flow out of the meat during cooking. This blood should be removed by sprinkling the meat with salt. The following is the procedure of salting:*

4. *Wash the meat well with water in order to remove all the blood on its surface, and then soak the meat in water for half-an-hour. Care should be taken that the meat be thoroughly submerged in the water and that the water covers the meat from all sides.*

5. *The wound on the neck where the foul has been slaughtered, and similarly any spot on the surface of the meat where the blood has hardened, should be thoroughly rubbed before soaking in order to remove the blood completely. And if there is a spot where the blood has collected in the flesh because of a blow or a wound then this spot should be cut and the blood removed before soaking. Removing the blood with water is not sufficient in this case.*

6. *Water which is very cold is unsuitable for soaking meat. It should be slightly warm before soaking.*

7. *Meat which has been left soaking in water for twenty-four hours is forbidden and can no longer be "kashered." The pot in which the meat has been soaked is also forbidden.*

8. *If liver has been left soaking in water for twenty-four hours, then the case should be referred to a competent rabbi.*

9.   *Frozen meat must first be warmed a little so as to un-freeze all the meat before soaking, but the meat should not be warmed in an oven or stove.*

10.   *The pot habitually used for soaking meat is not used for any other food. But a pot used only once for this purpose can be washed out thoroughly and used for normal purposes.*

11.   *After soaking the meat in water for half an hour, it should be removed and placed upon a special board or utensil, which is set aside for salting meat. In order to prevent the salt from being dissolved immediately, during salting, by the water on its surface, the meat should be set aside for a little while to enable the water to drip off.*

12.   *The salt used for salting should not be fine like flour for then it will dissolve immediately and not serve to draw the blood out of the meat. It should also not be too rough, for then it will fall off the meat. It should thus be of medium size.*

13.   *Sprinkle the salt on all the pieces of meat from all sides in order that no place should remain unsalted. When salting a fowl, it should first be opened in such a way as to enable the inside to be salted thoroughly as well.*

14.   *When salting meat at night care should be taken to leave no spot unsalted. A bright light should therefore be used.*

15.   *The meat should be left with the salt on it for a whole hour. On the eve of Sabbath, if one is pressed for time, twenty four minutes is sufficient (or even eighteen minutes, according to some authorities). Similarly, when pressed for time, one may shorten the period of soaking in water before salting, provided that one washes the meat and rubs it well with water before soaking.*

16.   *The board on which the meat is left with the salt on it, should be placed at a slant so that the blood can flow easily on to the ground, and not be contained at any point. In salting a chicken, hollow parts should be left with the hollow downwards so that the blood may flow freely.*

17.   *After the meat has been left with the salt on it for the appointed time, the salt should be shaken off the meat*

and completely removed, and thereafter the meat should be washed thoroughly three times. Before the salt has been washed off, it is forbidden to place this meat into an empty pot.

18. *In salting a fowl, care should be taken to remove the head before soaking and salting. If salting took place without removal of the head, the matter should be referred to a competent Rabbi.*

19. *The head of an animal or fowl should be cut open before soaking, and the brain should be first removed. The skin surrounding the brain should be torn and the brain soaked and salted on its own. If this has not been done, the matter should be referred to a competent Rabbi.*

20. *The head may be salted even though its hair is not removed.*

21. *It is customary to pass a small fire over the flesh of the fowl, after the feathers have been plucked, in order to burn off the thin hairs which remain. One should be careful to leave the fowl over the fire only a very short time, so that the fowl itself is not heated before being salted. Immediately after taking the fowl out of the fire it should be moved here and there in the wind in order to cool the skin.*

22. *One should break the wing of the fowl slightly, so that the blood can flow out at the time of salting.*

SALTING OF BONES, FEET AND HEART

1. *The bones attached to the meat are salted together with the meat; but once they have been separated from the meat they should be salted separately, and not be placed next to the meat with salt on.*

2. *The hooves should be removed from animals' feet before soaking and salting. The feet may be salted with the hair still attached.*

3. *The heart should be cut open first, and its blood removed before soaking and salting.*

4. *The lung should also be cut open before salting and the large veins should be opened.*

5. *Eggs found inside a hen, even if completely formed, should be soaked and salted as if they were meat. However they should be left with the salt on by themselves and not together with the meat.*

THE KASHERING OF LIVER

1. *The liver of an animal or fowl contains blood in large quantities and salting is therefore insufficient to prepare it for cooking. To prepare it for cooking or eating, the liver should be grilled over a fire or on red-hot coals.*

2. *Before grilling, the liver should be cut or perforated, and washed well in water. Thereafter it should be placed on the fire and sprinkled with salt while broiling. If salted before being placed on the fire, care should be taken not to leave it with its salt on it — it should immediately be put on the fire.*

3. *One is not allowed to grill the liver while it is wrapped in paper or something similar. The liver has to be directly on the fire, which draws the blood from it while it broils.*

4. *It is forbidden to salt the liver and leave it lying in its salt for a long time. It is all the more forbidden to leave a salted liver lying alongside salted meat. If this is done, a competent Rabbi should be consulted.*

5. *If the liver has been properly broiled, it may be cooked in a pot together with other meat.*

6. *One should not broil liver together with meat or fowl.*

VARIOUS LAWS CONCERNING SALTING

1. *Meat that has not yet been salted should not be put in a place where there might be some salt lying around. For salting makes the meat kosher for cooking only if properly done.*

2. *Meat left unsalted for three days may no longer be salted and cooked, and may only be eaten after being broiled. But if the meat was soaked in water during the three days, one is permitted to salt and cook it even after the three day period.*

3. *The teats of an animal may not be salted, but must be cut open cross-wise and then broiled over the fire.*

4. *The milt of an animal is salted just like ordinary meat, except that before soaking and salting, the skin, which is forbidden because of its fat, should be removed. It is also necessary to remove the sinews by drawing the main sinew out together with the three accompanying threads. Care should be taken not to tear any of the threads, for if a portion is left inside the milt, it must be cut out with a knife.*

BLOOD IN EGGS

1. *If a spot of blood is found in an egg, whether on the white or the yellow, the whole egg is forbidden.*

2. *If two eggs are boiled together and a spot of blood is found in one of them, then both eggs and the pot become forbidden. But if three eggs are boiled together and a spot of blood is found in one of them, the remaining two are permitted.*

3. *Boiled eggs may be eaten without having been inspected for a blood-spot. Nor is one obliged to inspect any egg which one is about to use, for most eggs have no blood in them. Nevertheless if the egg is opened before use, it is customary to see whether there is a blood-spot or not, if there is sufficient light.*

THE MIXING OF MEAT AND MILK

1. *The mixing of meat and milk is forbidden by the Torah. Not only the eating of milk and meat together, but even cooking them together is forbidden. If cooked together, whether on purpose or by accident, the product is forbidden for any use. One may not sell it to a non-Jew or give it to him as a present; nor may one derive any benefit from it, or make any use of it. It must simply be destroyed.*

2. *A pot or utensil which has absorbed a taste of milk and meat together is also forbidden. Thus a pot which has been used to cook milk, butter, cheese, or the like or in which milk has stood for twenty-four hours, may not be used for a meat-dish. For the milk-taste in the pot will enter the meat-*

dish and make it forbidden. Similarly a pot used to cook meat may not be used to cook any milk-dish.

3.   *For this reason every Jewish household should have two sets of table-ware and kitchen-ware, one set for milk products and the other for meat-products. It is also desirable to have a set of dishes used neither for meat-nor milk-products, for then what is cooked in these dishes may be served either with milk or with meat.*

4.   *The soap, straw, or steel-wool used to wash one set of dishes should not be used for the other, and these should be kept apart.*

5.   *Glass-ware not used for cooking does not absorb the taste of the food; thus if glass utensils are smooth and easily washable they can be used for both meat and milk-dishes.*

6.   *It is customary to mark the milk-set of dishes and pots and to leave the meat-set unmarked.*

7.   *It is forbidden to eat meat and milk one after the other. If one drinks milk, or cream or sour-milk, or eats light cheese or other milk foods, one may eat meat immediately after rinsing out one's mouth and washing one's hands, for milk foods do not leave traces in the mouth and their taste passes quickly.*

8.   *But if one eats meat or meat-foods, then one must wait six hours before eating milk foods, because of the particles of meat in one's teeth and the taste in one's mouth. Others wait only three or four hours. In this respect everyone should follow the customs of his parents.*

9.   *If one eats hard cheese or yellow cheese, one must wait, before eating meat foods, the same period of time that one normally waits between meat and milk. For the taste of hard or yellow cheese remains in the mouth for as long a period of time as the taste of meat.*

10.   *It is permitted to eat milk foods immediately after eating food cooked in pots usually used for meat, but in which there was no meat at all.*

11.   *Although it is allowed to eat meat immediately after all milk foods except hard or yellow cheese, one is not permitted to eat milk and meat as part of one and the same*

meal. A division must be made in the meal by saying grace after the milk portion, rearranging the table, and setting it a second time for the meat.

12.   Two friends or acquaintances may not sit at the same table if one of them eats milk food and the other meat-food, unless there is some division between the two of them, for example, two different table-cloths.

13.   If pots and pans, normally used for meat dishes, have accidentally been used for milk foods (or vice-versa), then the food cooked or fried in them is completely forbidden, and the utensil cannot be used for any cooking or frying until "kashered" as directed by a competent Rabbi. However the utensil may in the meantime be used for storing cold and dry fruits and vegetables.

14.   If cold milk falls into a boiling pot of meat-soup, or cold meat falls into a boiling pot of milk, or boiling meat falls into cold milk, or hot milk falls on cold meat, or both the meat and the milk are boiling — then in each of these cases a competent Rabbi must be consulted.

15.   If a drop of milk, whether hot or cold, falls on the outside of a pot of boiling meat, or falls on its lid, or similarly, if a drop of meat soup or gravy falls on the side or lid of a pot of hot milk, then too a competent Rabbi must be consulted.

16.   If a milk spoon or fork was accidentally put into hot meat, whether in the pot or on the plate, or if a meat spoon or fork was accidentally put into hot milk, or the wrong lid was put on the pot, if the food is warm then a competent Rabbi must be consulted. If everything was cold then one need only wash off the spoon, or fork.

17.   But if a meat knife was put into milk or vice-versa, then even when the food-stuff was cold, one must consult a competent Rabbi.

18.   Fish may be cooked in either meat or milk pots. But one may not mix meat with fish or cook them together.

19.   China-ware cannot be "kashered" and if made "treif," all china-ware is rendered unusable.

THE IMMERSION OF UTENSILS

1. *Metal or glass utensils made by a non-Jew, even when bought from a Jewish store, require ritual immersion in a Mikveh or in a river, or the sea, before being used.*

2. *Utensils used by a non-Jew or Jew who did not observe kashruth require "kashering" at the direction of a competent Rabbi.*

3. *New utensils made by a Jew never need ritual immersion, even if made by a Jew who does not observe kashruth.*

4. *On immersing utensils which require immersion, one first says the blessing, "Blessed art Thou, o Lord, our God, King of the Universe, who hath sanctified us with His commandments and commanded us concerning the immersion of utensils."*

5. *Earthenware pots or china-ware which are covered with lead require immersion, but no blessing is said before immersing them.*

6. *One is not allowed to immerse utensils on Sabbaths or holidays.*

THE PROHIBITION OF WORMS AND INSECTS

1. *There are four species of locusts which the Torah permits for food. But all other worms or insects, such as ants, bees, flies, and the like, are forbidden.*

2. *For this reason any foodstuff or drink which might contain worms, must first be carefully inspected for worms or worms' eggs. All worms or worms' eggs must be removed; and if it is not possible to remove them all, then the whole food or drink is forbidden.*

3. *Worms and insects are often to be found in figs, dry dates, plums, apricots and apples, and nuts. Oranges and grape fruits have worms at the end of the season. Flour which is not fresh needs careful sifting. Lettuce and cabbage require careful inspection. Lentils, beans and peas require inspection — every one which has a hole should be removed. Old Matzah requires inspection. One must be*

very careful with barley, oats and cereals which are not fresh. Water and vinegar, unless known to be pure, require straining. There are certain fish which have worms attached to their skin and heads at certain periods during the year, and one must learn how to inspect them.

GENERAL RULES CONCERNING "TREIFA"

1. If, on opening a chicken, one finds a nail or needle or something similar in one of the inner organs; or a perforation even without a nail; or finds the appearance of an internal organ changed because of some blow or wound; or finds blisters on the intestines; or finds the gall-bladder missing — then in each of these cases one must consult a competent Rabbi.

2. Similarly if one finds a leg or wing broken, a Rabbi should be consulted.

CHAPTER 21

■ THE PURE WELLSPRING (Taharath Hamishpachah)

"Observe therefore and do them: For this is your wisdom
and your understanding in the sight of the people, that, when
they hear all these statutes, shall say, 'surely this great nation
is a wise and understanding people!'" (Deut. 4:6).

FROM RIDICULE TO IMITATION

In antiquity the laws of the Torah were often the source of
ridicule. Thus, for many long years, the Gentiles mocked the
institution of the Sabbath. The Midrash describes a favorite pagan
amusement 2000 years ago:
"A corpse would be hauled into the amphitheater. A clown would
point to the body and ask the audience: 'Does anybody here know
why this man's face is pale and his head shaven?' To which another
clown would reply: 'Because the man's a Jew and Jews don't work
on Saturday. Whatever money they make during the week is
consumed by them on Saturday. They are therefore poor and have
no wood to cook with. To obtain wood they chop up their beds.
Since they have no beds to sleep on, they sleep on the ground.
They become soiled with dust, and their hair falls out. So they
annoint their heads with oil — and that is why oil is so expensive.'"

The audience would burst into gales of laughter at the Jews and their Sabbath. They could not see how it was possible to exist without working seven days a week.

Only gradually did the realization dawn on the Gentiles that a weekly day of rest was beneficial; eventually, the Gentiles imitated the Jews and instituted a compulsory weekly day of rest.

The same occurred with regard to circumcision. At first the Gentiles considered it a cruel custom. However, after many years of research and observation, medical authorities discovered the value of circumcision as a preventive of many dangerous diseases. In our time, circumcision is performed as a matter of course in many countries.

ONE SHEEP IN THE MIDST OF SEVENTY WOLVES

The continued existence of the Jewish people, faithfully observing its Torah and stubbornly preserving its separate identity, has always seemed, in the estimate of the nations of the world, a strange phenomenon with no hope of lasting endurance.

Amongst the world's peoples there were some who expected the process of assimilation to reduce the differentiation of Jewish life, and to gradually lead to the disappearance of Jewish identity. In some places it has been said of the Jewish people: 'Come and let us cut them off from being a nation; that the name of Israel may be no more in remembrance' (Psalms 35:5).

Assimilation has withered many limbs of the Jewish people, and the Hamans and Hitlers of the ages have wrought terrible devastation amongst us. But the people of Israel has survived both threats and will live unto eternity!

How could so small and poor a nation survive, and even emerge ascendant in the face of all the forces seeking its destruction?

Some amongst the wise of the nations have perceived it, while we have known it as a testimony of the Torah: 'surely this great nation is a wise and understanding people' (Deut. 4:6). The life of the Jewish people is not subject to the same laws which govern the life of other nations. The laws of the Torah are the laws of its survival.

THE MIRROR OF GENERATIONS

The Torah's wisdom is not always revealed by logical analysis. Oft times, only history reveals its wisdom. And since history is not yet a finished process, the revelation of the Torah's wisdom remains incomplete. What has hitherto been revealed is no more than a faint glimmer of a light whose brilliance is capable of illuminating the entire universe. The matter may be compared to a son of the desert who, upon reaching the outskirts of civilization, is amazed at the sight of primitive huts and shacks. The people he sees in those primitive abodes seem wondrous to him; the clothes they wear, the tables they eat at, the homes they inhabit — all seem so impressive. How much more amazement will our desert dweller feel, when he arrives at a large city and sees genuinely beautiful clothes, genuinely palatial residences, genuinely lavish food, and pleasures of which he never dreamt.

The full beauty and wisdom of the Torah has not yet been revealed. What little of its contents has begun to be understood, is rapidly gaining the acknowledgement and respect of the nations of the world. The largest part of the Torah however, still remains uncomprehended. Only history will increase our understanding of its treasured contents. As for the Jewish people, its wisdom consists in the unconditional trust it has reposed in the Torah. The effects of the observance of the Torah are immediately visible, whereas an understanding of its inner wisdom may be revealed only generations hence. The fool alone will say, 'I shall accept the law only after I see its results.' If everyone were to behave thus, the farmer would not sow, the patient would not take medicine, the pupil would not listen to his teacher. The world could not endure. True wisdom requires love of even concealed wisdom, and true understanding entails the ability to anticipate ends from beginnings. Such wisdom is the heritage of the Jewish people who said at Sinai, 'We shall observe and we shall hearken!'

PURITY — THE FOUNDATION OF MARRIAGE

Married life must be pure, and the laws of purity set forth in the Torah are the fundamental principles of wedlock.

The separation of husband and wife enjoined during the menstrual period is one of the three basic injunctions in the Torah which must be observed, even if the alternative is death. It is included under the head of sexual immorality; the other two are idolatry and bloodshed. The observance of this rigorous separation during menstruation is one of the distinguishing marks of Jewish family life, setting the Jewish people apart from their Gentile neighbors and preventing assimilation.

UNANSWERED QUESTIONS

"It is obvious and evident that purity and impurity are divine decrees, not matters discernible by the human mind . . . Immersion after the period of menstrual impurity is over is not merely a question of removing the remains of the flow by washing — it is a divine decree. What is involved is not a question of hard fact, but of the heart's devotion." (Maimonides, end of commentary on the treatise of Mikvaoth.)

Since the laws respecting menstruation constitute a divine decree, and are not matters of human regulation, questioning of the details of the separation of husband and wife are pointless. Why does an emission of blood, or a certain-colored stain render the wife impure, while a stain of another color does not? Why does the wife have to count seven days free of bleeding? Why is the water of the mikveh suitable for immersion, and not a bath or shower? Why must all the hair be immersed, or the immersion is invalid?

These questions are not directly answerable. The knowledge remains ours however, that this law is given to us by the same Creator who imprinted His laws on the whole of Creation. It is as much a law of nature for the Jewish people to observe God's commandments as it is for fire to ascend, dust to settle, one end of a magnet to attract, the other to repel, the earth and planets to remain in their fixed orbits.

SCIENTIFIC DISCOVERIES

The experience of ages and scientific research have confirmed the tangible medical benefits of menstrual separation. Investigation has discovered that the menstrual blood contains a harmful element capable of producing adverse effects on cells with weak resistance. It has also been found that observance of the Jewish purity laws offers complete safeguard against a number of women's and children's diseases.

These findings, though reassuring to the believing Jew, add nothing to the essential significance of our laws of purity. We observe them, as we do all the other laws in the Torah, not for their "practical" benefits, but because they are divine commandments.

AS A LAW OF NATURE

If menstrual separation were practised by the Jewish people

because of the recommendation of the many medical authorities who currently recommend such separation, human nature might militate against the constancy of such practice. For, human nature is so constituted that the soundest of medical advice often fails to prevail against the temptation of instinct and inconvenience. Such advice is best heeded, where reward is immediately tangible and exceeds the inconvenience entailed. Where however, such reward is intangible and distant, while inconvenience is immediate, and pleasure beckons on the other hand, then medical advice often goes unheeded.

What cannot be assured in the absence of police and law courts, can however be assured through the sense of obedience to Divine commandment which attends the observance of the laws of menstrual separation on the part of the Jewish people. These laws are for us laws of nature, whose transgression brings in its wake inevitable retribution, just as casting oneself into a fire does. The Jewish people needs no policemen to enforce observance of the law. It observes the law as a matter of course, in awareness of the folly of allowing satisfaction of transient desire to cause it the loss of this world and the next, its own world and the world of its descendants.

ISRAEL'S VIEW OF THE FUTURE

When husband and wife marry, they enter a relationship of infinitely larger import than a commercial agreement for the fulfillment of mutual need or desire. Theirs should be a sense of entering into a covenant binding to eternity; a covenant whose effects will reach all the generations to be descended from them. The garden they plant at the hour of marriage, will produce seed long after they themselves will have ceased to be. If their beginnings are right they may harbor glowing hope for the generations to follow, otherwise, their seed will grow weeds which will inflict harm on their descendants. At the hour of marriage, a husband and wife ought to be aware of the wisdom and strength transmitted to them by their own ancestors, so that they might know how to direct their own offspring along paths whose safety is proven, rather than along paths filled with obstacles and snares.

A person who is completely self-centered detaches himself from the line of succession which leads from his ancestors to his descendants. A person who lives only for the present, is unable to prevail against the temptations of the moment.

If one however, regards himself as a link in the chain of generations, he will cherish the achievement of his ancestors as a gain for the present, and a cherished treasure to be zealously guarded and passed on to the future. He will view all his actions as his contributions to eternity. The good inherited from yesterday lights his way today; the bad remains an irksome obstacle placed in his path. The good he does today will light his way tomorrow, the bad will be an obstacle in the path of his future. For him, yesterday, today and tomorrow form an eternal unity which will never pass away. For him, the past is never lost, the future never inscrutable — everything is revealed, alive and present. One who lives his life in this awareness will ever be able to withstand momentary temptation, however great. For, will he allow momentary pleasure to outweigh eternal regret?

The fountain from which all the generations of the Jewish people draw sustenance, is pure and clear; and every Jew should be constantly aware of the toil and labor his ancestors expended to preserve the purity of that fountain. Every Jewish person should realize that he, in turn, is charged with the preservation of that purity. Shall he be the one to set at naught the efforts of his ancestors and, irresponsibly, cast stain and blemish on his future? Shall he not tremble lest he defile his own children?

The commandments concerning the purity of the Jewish family are enjoined upon every Jewish couple, with utmost severity. For, while the practice of those commandments bestows merit upon ancestors and descendants alike, their violation casts reflection not only upon those who commit such violation, but also on their ancestors and descendants.

COMPASSION FOR DESCENDANTS

Since the purity of family life is so important a part of Jewish life, even Jews who have been more or less estranged from the traditions of their forefathers have felt obliged to observe the purity laws as a matter of course. And this is as it should be. For in the case of many other laws, breaking them affects the transgressor alone — breaking the purity laws injures one's children irremediably.

Parental love for children is proverbial. A child who begs with all his heart for something his father knows is not really necessary usually gets his way, because his father does not want to hurt his feelings. On the point of death, mothers think only of their children's grief, not of themselves. It is unimaginable for parents, for a brief moment of pleasure, to bring grief to their unborn children, except out of ignorance of the dire consequences. Let us admit, for the sake of argument that the parents regard themselves as enlightened and scoff at their ancestors' "taboos." But what if their children should return to the traditions of their forefathers. Can we fail to see that our people, together with a large part of humanity, stands at the threshold of an age of renewed faith? Do we not see everywhere about us a profound yearning and a quest for God in the rising generation? Are there not, in our time, frequent instances of children born to non-observant Jewish parents who wholeheartedly embrace the way of life of their forefathers? What a sense of tragedy is felt by such children, when they become aware that their parents have neglected the rules of family purity! Ought not every Jewish parent see to it, that no such tragedy occur in the family he is building?

Let not a Jewish parent "take refuge" in his being non-observant of Jewish law, and think that the likelihood of his children's returning to the practices of Jewish tradition is therefore non-existent, or only a remote possibility, because of the upbringing he gave them. Quite the contrary. For loyalty to God and His mitzvoth, is imbedded in the deepest recesses of Jewish being. However far generations stray from the Jewish tradition, adversity brings them back in regret and repentance. This is one of the most dramatic processes discernible in the history of the Jewish people. New ideas are quickly embraced by Jewish youth, which is always an intellectually inclined youth. They become estranged from Judaism; they want to be "modern" and "enlightened." A generation or two passes and the grandchildren of these parents wrestle with the problem of their Jewish identity. They face the prospect of total assimilation and intermarriage with their Gentile neighbors. Some take the path of least resistance, others seek to strengthen their Jewish ties. At such times, winds of hostility or anti-Semitism often spark a wholesale renewal of Jewish identification and a strengthening of Jewish tradition. So it is — so it will be.

No matter how non-observant you may be, or how "heretic" be your opinions, be prepared for the fact that your children may turn away from your violation of the Torah, just as you, or your parents once turned away from observance of Torah. If you do not observe the rules of family purity, they will one day despise you in their hearts for casting a stain upon them. Know, therefore, that if you have marital relations during menstruation, or before the visit to the mikveh, you may be causing your children untold pain. Do not be cruel to your children!

A PERSON IS BORN TO STRIVE

But why burden ourselves with the commandments? Why not do as we like and enjoy life to its full, without restrictions?

This is not a wise thought. Man's superiority over the beasts, lies in the fact that he bears a greater burden. Whatever he achieves involves hard work. All the other creatures were created to serve man; his burden of labor leads to greatness.

This applies to reproduction as well as to every other phase of life. All the other creatures reproduce themselves painlessly — man alone enters the world attended by great pain. This is because the birth of every human being is an event of importance, while the birth of any individual animal has no special significance. When a calf, or a sheep, or a goat is born, its particular birth is unimportant. The barrenness of the individual animal is more than compensated by the fertility of the rest of the species. All animals are equal in value — no one of them has any special meaning.

Not so with man. Though the world be crowded with human beings, the birth of a child is always a noteworthy event — no one knows what great things may not come from this child. Human barrenness is a tragedy, involving a potential loss to the whole world. Sarah, Rebecca, Rachel, and Hannah were all barren at first. Had they not eventually borne children, what a loss that would have been to the world!

That is why the birth of a child is both accompanied by pain and a noteworthy event. With each birth a new light shines in the world, a new crown graces the glory of mankind.

There is one other respect in which the human mother and child are quite different from their animal counterparts. No other creature has a menstrual flow. This is because the creation of a new human life is like the creation of a new world, and the conditions attendant to birth must always be fresh and new.

THE MONTHLY CYCLE-RENEWAL

The menstrual cycle suggests a profound symbolism. The Jewish month is a lunar month. Renewal and rebirth are processes which peculiarly characterize Jewish existence, and the waxing and waning of the moon have always represented to the Jew the processes which he notes as operative throughout Jewish history. The moon wanes smaller and smaller — it even vanishes to the eye. But this is only a prelude to a rebirth after which it will wax larger and larger till it reaches its fullness. Similarly with the Jewish people; no matter how much they are harassed and decimated, no matter how much they dwindle in strength and numbers, they retain the assurance of renewal.

This peculiar power of rebirth which has been given to the Jewish people sustains it in life, and assures its eternal survival. Other nations rise, achieve greater and greater strength, until they reach a certain point. But once they reach that point they fall and never regain their earlier stature. They dwindle until they vanish altogether. Not so the Jewish people!

Fifteen generations, from Abraham to King Solomon, the Jewish people rose and continued on the ascent. For fifteen generations, from Rehoboam till Zedekiah it fell and experienced descent, till it reached the lowest rung of degradation. All its enemies lifted their heads in gladness, anticipating Israel's imminent final downfall and total extinction. It seemed that the light of Israel would be extinguished forever. But behold, there was a new rebirth, like the rebirth of the moon. The light of Israel waxed again. It shone forth in exile and it shone forth again in the land of Israel, and it has continuously renewed itself from that day to this. Even though this light is sometimes covered, it is never extinguished. And the continual renewal of the light of the moon is a symbol for Israel that its own light will never be extinguished and that it is destined to renew its youthful vigor.

The greatness of woman consists in the fact that the Almighty gave this same power of rebirth, which He imprinted upon the soul of the Jewish nation, to her. Woman renews her strength every month, as the moon renews its light monthly. She renews her essential powers, her capacity for fruitfulness, the power of her youthful love, her attractiveness to her husband.

The Jewish woman who observes the laws of purity, separates herself at the proper time and purifies herself at the proper time, is as beloved to her husband as on the day of their marriage. Her life with her husband is one of everlasting love and respect. They will never tire of each other. They erect a fence of roses between themselves when marital relations are forbidden, and during this period the flame of desire is replaced by the moral superiority of the spirit, which restrains desire through fear of sin. For man's spirit has no greater moment of glory that when it completely controls his personality. When a man is controlled by his desires, he is filled with feelings of remorse and shame; but when he rules over his desires, his soul is full of pride and splendor, and he always feels content, happy and secure.

When one masters one's desires even once, he rejoices and is greatly rewarded both in this world and world to come. How much more do a Jewish husband and wife rejoice, who master their desires all their days. How great is their reward! For, they experience a continual renewal of their love and a continual freshness and delight in their conjugal relations.

The strength of the Jewish family has ever been the marvel and the envy of the nations. The wise and the righteous among the nations have always sung hymns of praise to the peace and freshness of Jewish family life, whereas the foolish and the wicked have been driven by their envy to deeds of hatred and enmity towards the Jewish people. Amongst the practices of Judaism which our enemies have attempted to suppress, the observance of family purity has ranked first. Therein, they paid unwilling tribute to the part which the rules of family purity have always played in investing the Jewish family with its enduring strength.

PURIFICATION THROUGH THE WATERS OF CREATION

It has already been said that no reasons are necessary to support the commandments of the Torah and that these should be regarded as royal decrees. They are more valuable to us when we do not know their reasons, for then we observe them simply out of the love of God and not for any other motive. Thus nothing of the significance of the commandment that purification should take place only in a mikveh (ritual bath) or natural spring, is lost because of the fact that no reason is given for this in the Torah.

Although no reason is directly given for immersion in a mikveh, the Torah does hint at the symbolism of ritual immersion. Emergence from the mikveh is like being re-created, in a new creation where nothing has yet become impure. At the beginning of God's creation of the world, everything was water and the spirit of the Lord hovered above the surface of the waters. Until the Lord said: "Let the waters under the heaven be gathered together unto one place, and let the dry land appear." (Genesis 1, 9.) At that moment the whole of creation, the land and all upon it were clean and pure without any vestige of sin or impurity.

Ritual immersion consists of submerging oneself completely in waters which are found on the earth by Divine decree — waters of a natural spring, or rain-water ingathered on the ground, in a natural or artificially-formed pit (of fixed specifications). The immersion has to be complete with not a single hair left unsubmerged, at which time there is a symbolical reversion to the moment when the waters of creation covered the depths and the spirit of the Lord hovered above the surface of the waters.

One emerges from these waters purified and renewed, as if newly created, with all one's earlier impurities cleansed and washed away.

Thus all the drawn water in the world, and all the bathtubs or showers do not purify. Even the natural waters of creation do not purify unless they cover the body completely. Only a ritual bath fulfilling all the specifications can purify.

MOTHERS AND DAUGHTERS

Since the laws of family purity are laws of life to those who observe them, for themselves and for their descendants; since they are rules which affect the very foundation of Jewish existence, it is not surprising that Jewish women in all ages observed these rules with an exemplary devotion, equalled only by the legendary heroes of history.

Jewish women from far-flung settlements used to travel regularly days on end in order to reach a place which had a mikveh and purify themselves. In some places where there was no mikveh, women risked their lives immersing themselves in rivers or the sea, in dangerous circumstances. And many were the Jewish women who for want of any other means of purifying themselves, used to hack holes in the ice covering rivers which had been frozen over during the cold winter, and immerse themselves in the icy waters. Women who were prevented by circumstances from immersing themselves, willingly lived for years separated from their husbands rather than transgress even once the commandments of God.

These are your mothers, Israel! These are your mothers. And blessed may they be for having preserved us and sustained us in life till this day. Were it not for them and their heroism, for their devotion to the pure fountain of our people's life waters there would, God forbid, have been no remnant left of the Jewish people, weak and hated as it was. It was they who gave eternity to the Jewish people!

It is therefore unimaginable that Jewish women in our day should break down the boundaries which their mothers have built, and bring, God forbid, catastrophe upon themselves, their husbands and their children, and destruction upon the whole of the Jewish people. The gratification of the moment is certainly not worth injury inflicted upon parents, upon children and the whole Jewish people.

Our enemies have for ages tried to destroy us and failed. Shall we then bring destruction upon ourselves, by removing the foundation stone on which our eternal existence rests, by breaking down the wall which has served as the bastion of defense for Jewish survival, by selling out the Jewish soul to the domain of passions and desires?

And of those whose shallow "enlightenment" does not allow them to see things as they are, we ask that they picture their children standing before them and demanding from them: "Why did you not give us the freedom of choice, that you yourselves received from your parents? Why did you stain us from birth? Why?" We feel sure that Jewish parents desire to give to their children the opportunities that they themselves have received from their forebears; that they do not wish to deprive their children of their freedom of choice before they are born. Let it be said then to all Jewish parents: "Allow your children to grow up free to choose for themselves the path on which they wish to go."

For this reason, every Jewish woman is bidden to observe all the details of the laws of family purity. Let her honor these rules and observe them with pride, disregarding the folly of those who scoff at her because of it. The scoffers destroy the Jewish people, whereas she contributes to its survival.

To the Jewish woman who observes the laws of family purity, we may apply the verse: "Observe therefore and do them, for this is your wisdom and your understanding in the sight of the peoples, that when they hear all these statutes, shall say: 'Surely this great nation is a wise and understanding people.'" (Deut. 4:6.)

■ WHEN INTERCOURSE BECOMES FORBIDDEN

1. *A woman is considered a "Niddah" (i.e. in her period of separation) and intercourse with her husband is forbidden (Lev. 20, 18), when even one drop of blood, the size of a grain of mustard, is emitted from her womb, regardless of whether the omission occurs at the normal period of menstruation or not, or during pregnancy or when she is nursing. Relations with her husband are thereupon forbidden until she purifies herself in the prescribed manner (which we shall presently discuss).*

2. *Any type of blood which is secreted, whether bright or dark or even black, pink or any other reddish color, makes her a "Niddah." But the emission of any liquid which is definitely not red in color, does not make her a "Niddah." If there is some doubt whether the color is reddish or not, a competent Rabbi should be consulted.*

3. *A woman who feels the womb opening as it normally does when she menstruates, or who feels herself emitting something even if she did not previously feel the womb opening, and thereupon examines herself immediately and finds the color of the emission definitely non-reddish, does not become a "Niddah." But if she examined herself immediately and found nothing, or if she waited some time before examining herself, and found either nothing or an emission definitely non-reddish in color, she should consult a competent Rabbi. (such consultation may be indirect, by telephone or a third person.)*

4. *If a pregnant woman after her third month feels the womb opening or the flow of fluid, and on immediate examination she finds the emission definitely non-reddish in color, or she finds nothing at all, then she does not become a "Niddah."*

5. *A woman, not in her menstrual period, who finds on*

her flesh or clothing or sheet, a stain which looks like blood or is golden or wax-like in color, or

6. *If she noticed blood in her urine, or*

7. *If blood flows as the result of a medical examination, she should consult a competent Rabbi.*

8. *For the whole of the night or day (from sunrise to sunset) during which the menstruation is expected to begin (in the event of there being a regular and fixed menstrual period), her husband must not approach her even if there has been no emission of blood and no stain and she has not felt the womb opening or the flow of fluid. A regular menstrual period can be fixed in one of the four following ways:*

(i) *If the three previous menstruations began on the same day of the Jewish calendar month, the next menstruation may be expected to begin on the same day of the next month, and the husband may have no relations with her during the whole of that day.*

(ii) *If her previous menstruations began after a regular interval of days from each other, and this occured consecutively three times, then it is considered probable that this will occur a fourth time, and during the whole day following the regular interval, relations with her husband are forbidden.*

(iii) *If the interval of days between one menstruation and another is increased or decreased in a regular pattern; for example, if the five previous menstruations occurred at the following intervals: the second 28 days after the first, the third 29 days after the second, the fourth 30 days after the third, and the fifth 31 days after the fourth, so that there have been three intervals constantly increasing by one day, then the next menstruation (i.e. the sixth) may be expected 32 days after the previous one (i.e. the fifth) and on the whole of that day relations between husband and wife are forbidden.*

Similarly a decreasing regular interval could be fixed, if the interval between the first and second was 31 days, between the second and third 30 days, between

the third and fourth 29 days, and between the fourth
and fifth 28 days. In this case the next menstruation
could be expected to begin on the 27th day, and for
the whole of that day relations between husband and
wife would be forbidden.

(iv) If the three previous menstruations occurred in the
same circumstances; for example, if the beginning of
the flow was each time preceded by a yawn (or
sneeze, or sensation of heaviness of the limbs, shiver
of the knees, nausea, etc.), then when the same circumstance, or circumstances recur for the fourth time,
it is probable that the menstrual flow will begin, and
relations between husband and wife are forbidden
for the whole day.

In some cases the regular menstrual period is fixed
by a combination of two of the above methods
together, for example, some bodily circumstances
(a yawn, etc.) and a fixed day in the month (or fixed
interval). In such cases, when the two symptoms have
occurred together three times, menstruation may be
expected to occur when the two symptoms recur together a fourth time, and relations between husband
and wife are then forbidden for the whole day.

9. Once fixed, the regular menstrual period remains in
force legally until three consecutive menstruations occur
at times other than the regular period. In such a case her
period is regarded as irregular and the rules contained in
the next paragraph apply to her.

10. Where there is no regular period, or where a regular
period formerly fixed has become irregular, and no new
regular period has been fixed, or her period is known to
fall on one of 3-4 days but not on any of them in particular,
or where a woman has once or twice experienced emissions
of blood between her regular periods — in all these cases
a competent Rabbi should be consulted.

11. If the expected day of menstruation passed by
without the menstruation beginning, no further separation between husband and wife is required. After the wife
has examined herself, they may have relations with each
other.

12.   *A woman who has become a "Niddah" in any of the days mentioned in paragraphs 1-7 is forbidden to have relations with her husband, no matter how much time has elapsed or how many baths she has had, until she becomes "pure" (i.e. permitted) in the manner prescribed by the law. This process of purification consists of five steps: (i) she waits until the days of "impurity" have ended; (ii) she performs the "transition to purity; (iii) she counts seven days; (iv) she examines herself in the pre-scribed manner during these seven days; (v) she immerses herself in a "Mikveh." The details of these five steps will be explained in subsequent sections.*

THE DAYS OF "IMPURITY"

1.   *If a woman has become "impure" (i.e. forbidden to have relations with her husband) in any of the possible ways of becoming impure (for example by finding or feeling the flow of blood; or finding a stain of a reddish color even without specially looking for it or having been aware of its emission, or by feeling the sensation of the opening of the womb or the emission of fluid (as above sub-section 3) then even if she sees or experiences nothing further after the sight or experience which made her "impure," she must count a minimum of five days of "impurity" just as if she were seeing or experiencing the flow of blood all this time. (There are other authorities who require a count of six days for blood and five for stains). These five days are a minimum, and if bleeding or staining continues after this period then the days of "impurity" extend until the flow stops.*

2.   *No matter what time of the day (counted from sunset till sunset) the bleeding or staining occurred, that day (even though less than a full day) counts as the first of the five days. Thus even if the bleeding occurred a little before sunset that is counted as the first day, and the evening is already the evening of the second day of the five.*

THE "TRANSITION TO PURITY" (HEFSEK TAHARAH)

1.   *After the five-day (or more) period of "impurity" is over, the woman is required to count seven days clear of*

bleeding or staining before she may resume relations with her husband. This seven-day period must *be preceded by a special inspection which is called the "transition to purity" (hefsek taharah).*

2. *This special inspection is made in the following manner: At the end of her five-day (or more) period of impurity, just before sunset, the vagina and the whole area between her thighs must be thoroughly washed with warm water (and the whole body bathed if possible). She should thereafter put on clean underwear (or if she has none, thoroughly inspect her previous underclothes and see to it that there should be no stain). Before dressing herself she should take a piece of clean white cottonwool or linen (if soft) and insert it with her finger into the vaginal canal, pushing it as far as she can. She should move and turn the cottonwool in all directions and then take it out and inspect it by daylight. If there is no stain of blood and the cottonwool is completely clean the "transition to purity" may begin, and she begins to count the seven days from that evening.*

3. *If for some reason she did not make the inspection at all, or did not inspect properly, then she may* not *begin counting that evening and must wait till a little before sunset of the next day and then make the "transition to purity." Only thereafter does she start counting the seven days.*

4. *If on removing the cotton-wool from the vagina a stain is found, she should immediately wash herself a second time and make a second inspection. If the cotton-wool is now clean and without any stain, the "transition to purity" begins and she may begin to count the seven-day period from the evening.*

5. *It is recommended that, immediately after the inspection which marks the "transition to purity" has been completed, she should insert a clean piece of cotton-wool deep into the vagina and leave it there till night-fall. She should then remove it, put it aside, and inspect by daylight the following morning.*

6. *After making the "transition to purity," she should*

change her bed-linen and put on clean sheets. (If she has none, then she must inspect the sheets carefully to see that there are no stains.)

THE SEVEN "CLEAN" DAYS

1.   *After the "transition to purity" seven whole days must elapse before she is permitted to her husband. These days are reckoned from sunset to sunset, so that she starts counting the first after the sunset during which the inspection of the "transition to purity" took place, and the seven days end after the sunset of the seventh day.*

2.   *On each of these seven days she must make a thorough examination of herself, the same examination as she made for her "transition to purity," twice a day, once in the morning and once before sunset, so that she can both times inspect the cotton-wool by daylight.*

3.   *The thorough examinations on the first day and the seventh day are indispensable, and if one of them was omitted or not properly made, a competent Rabbi should be consulted. The inspections on the intermediate five days are necessary, but if one or all of them have been omitted this does not invalidate the seven-day counting, so long as the examinations of the first and seventh days have been carried out.*

4.   *If at any time during these seven days she finds blood or a stain, then she has to start the seven days all over again after making another "transition to purity" inspection before the sunset of the day on which the renewed bleeding or staining stops. There is no need to count five days of "impurity" in this case.*

5.   *If her "transition to purity" inspection falls on the Sabbath or a Festival or on the Day of Atonement, then she should wash the whole of the area between her thighs in cold water or in water heated the previous day. She should not use any sponge or cloth for the washing, for pressing water out of a sponge or cloth is forbidden on a Sabbath or Festival.*

6.   *If her "transition to purity" inspection falls due while*

167

she is in her seven days of mourning for her nearest relative, she may wash herself in the normal way.

LAWS OF RITUAL IMMERSION

After the seven days have passed, without her finding any blood or stain, she is forbidden to her husband until she has ritually immersed herself, in the proper way, in a "Mikveh." No amount of washing in a bathtub, a shower, or in any other manner will suffice. Even if she goes to a "Mikveh" but does not immerse herself properly, relations with her husband are as forbidden as on the days of her menstrual flow.

The following are the regulations concerning ritual immersion in a Mikveh:

1. Towards evening, on the seventh day, she should go to the Mikveh, remove all her rings, bracelets and jewelry as well as false teeth and anything similar. She should cut her finger-nails and toe-nails and wash herself thoroughly in hot water, paying particular attention to the area between her thighs and to all the folds in her skin. Nose, ears, her navel, and the area between the fingers should be thoroughly cleaned. She should brush her teeth and rinse out her mouth. She should wash her head with soap and water (but not too much soap), comb out the hair on her head and body until she is sure that none are stuck together. She should wash slowly and unhurriedly until the stars emerge.

After the stars have emerged and she has completed washing herself thoroughly, she should inspect her whole body once more to be sure that there is nothing on it that should prevent the water of the Mikveh from reaching her body, and with her body still moist from washing, she should descend the Mikveh to immerse herself. All the time that she has been busy washing and preparing herself, till after the actual immersion itself, she should not eat anything. If she walks barefoot from the bath to the Mikveh she should again examine the soles of her feet, for they may have become dirty through walking over the floor. If so she should wash them again before descending into the Mikveh.

She should immerse herself in the Mikveh until the water reaches the level of her heart, and then bend down easily, like a mother bending over a cradle, so that the water covers her whole body, her head and her hair, with not a single hair left uncovered.

The water should be able to penetrate all parts of her body including folds of her skin. For this reason she should not close her lips too tightly; she need not open them either, but just hold them against each other freely. She should not close her eyes tightly, clench her fists tightly, nor hold her legs together tightly. Her arms and legs should be as when she is walking in the street. Her arms should be held a little away from the body and her legs slightly apart. She should not immerse herself standing bolt upright, nor sitting, but bending easily, as we have described.

After remaining a little while with all her body and hair submerged she can lift her head out of the water and stand up straight. She should fold her arms below her heart, lift her eyes upwards, and, while still in the water, pronounce the blessing: "Blessed art Thou, o Lord, our God, King of the Universe, Who hath sanctified us with His commandments, and commanded us concerning ritual immersion." Then she should immerse herself a second time, in exactly the same fashion as before. She then emerges from the water purified and ready to resume relations with her husband.

2. An adult Jewish woman should be present at the time of the immersion in order to see that the immersion has been done in the proper manner and that not a single hair of her head has remained outside the water.

3. The following things make the immersion invalid:

If she immersed herself on the seventh day before the stars came out; if she immersed herself without washing herself before immersion; if there was something on her body which prevented the water covering her completely, or if her hair were stuck together; if she washed herself without inspecting her body to see that no foreign body or dirt was left on it which might prevent the water reaching all parts of her skin, the immersion is invalid even if she inspects herself after immersion and finds nothing on her body; if she did not comb her hair before immersion, or if she combed them when they were dry, even if she washed them afterwards, the immersion is invalid; if she closed her lips tightly or closed her eyes tightly, pressed her fingers or toes together tightly, or clenched her fists tightly, then the immersion is invalid; if any part of her body was not covered by the water, even if it was only a single hair. If she immersed herself in the water standing bolt upright, she should immerse herself a second time properly. If she held the ends of her hair in her mouth then the immersion is invalid.

4.   *If her husband is in town, she is not allowed to delay her visit to the Mikveh, but should immerse herself immediately after her seven days in which there has been no flow. Similarly her husband is not allowed to absent himself from the house on the night of her visit to the Mikveh unless it is absolutely unavoidable.*

5.   *In case of necessity or when her husband is out of town she can delay her visit to the Mikveh for a day. But whenever she goes, her immersion should take place after nightfall (i.e. after the stars have come out).*

6.   *If she did not visit the Mikveh at the end of the seventh day, and cannot under any circumstances wait till after nightfall of the eighth day before immersing herself, then she may immerse herself during the day in the utmost secrecy but should not let her husband know about it till after nightfall.*

7.   *It is advisable not to eat meat on the day before the visit to the Mikveh, for pieces of meat enter between the teeth very easily and it is very difficult to remove them before the immersion. But this should not prevent her eating meat on Sabbaths and Festivals in the normal way, if the seventh day falls on one of these. She should however make a point of picking her teeth and cleaning them well before immersing herself.*

8.   *It is very commendable to begin washing while it is still day and to continue doing so till nightfall and then immerse oneself immediately. But if she cannot manage to do the washing during the day, then she may wash and*

immerse herself in the evening, so long as she does not hurry over this.

9.   *If the night of her visit to the Mikveh falls on Sabbath Eve or on the Eve of a Festival, she should wash during the day because it is forbidden to do many things connected with washing on Sabbath or on a Festival.*

10.   *When washing herself on the eve of Sabbath, it is better to ask her husband to light the Sabbath candles at home while she goes about her washing unhurriedly and immerses herself after nightfall, rather than that she should hurry with her washing, rush home to light candles and return to the Mikveh to immerse herself after nightfall.*

11.   *A woman may light the Sabbath candles at home long before Sabbath begins, and then proceed to the Mikveh to remain there till after nightfall. When she lights the candles she must however explicitly say, "I do not wish Sabbath to begin for me until the proper time" before she makes the blessing over lighting the candles and proceeds to the Mikveh. She must use longer candles than usual, in order that they should burn till night.*

12.   *If her visit to the Mikveh should fall due on a Saturday night, right after Sabbath — she should wash herself thoroughly before the Sabbath, and examine her body carefully before immersing herself after the Sabbath. It is also proper that she should wash herself again before immersion.*

If her visit to the Mikveh falls on the evening between the first and second days of a Festival or between the second day of a Festival, which falls on a Friday, and the Sabbath which follows immediately after it, then the main washing and preparations should be done on the afternoon before the first day of the Festival (i.e. on Wednesday afternoon in the case where the two days of the Festival fall on Thursday and Friday).

During the Festival, the woman should take particular care not to get her hair dirty or ruffled — she should keep it covered all the time. When washing before the Festival she should wash herself with special care, and throughout the Festival she should pay special attention to keeping her hands clean and to letting nothing stick to them. She should wash them immediately whenever dirtied. Before immersing herself, at the appointed time, she should examine her whole body and hair thoroughly and rinse out her mouth and teeth. The folds of her body should be washed with water kept warm from before the Festival, if such water is available. Teeth should be picked and every particle of food removed.

13. *It is desirable that she should wash herself at the Mikveh just before she immerses herself. If, however, she has washed herself elsewhere, she should bring along a comb to the Mikveh and comb her hair a second time before the immersion.*

14. *A woman whose hair is long, or who has no one to supervise and tell her if all her hair is under water may cover her hair with a very loose net.*

15. *Some women feel they need to hold the hand of a helper in order to feel secure while immersing themselves. In these cases, the helper should first dip her own hand into the Mikveh and then hold the hand of the woman entering the water very loosely.*

16. *After she emerges from the Mikveh and while still in the bath-house, she is not allowed to bathe either in a bathtub or in a shower, or even pour hot water over her body from some utensil. But when she returns to her home all of these become permissible.*

17. *It is customary for a woman emerging from the Mikveh to be greeted and touched by a woman who has been in the Mikveh before her.*

18. *A woman should not divulge the date or fact of her immersion in the Mikveh to anyone except her husband.*

19. *The following cases require the advice of a competent Rabbi:*

If the woman concerned is in the habit of manicuring her nails and growing them long; if she has a temporary filling in her teeth; or wounds on her skin; if she returns home from the Mikveh and finds something stuck to her skin.

In all these cases, and, in general, in all cases of doubt, no woman should decide the issue herself, but should consult a competent Rabbi.

MAIN LAWS CONCERNING PREGNANT AND NURSING WOMEN

1. *A woman who has been pregnant for three months and a woman nursing her child are regarded as unlikely to see blood. They need keep no account of their previous menstrual periods and are permitted to their husbands without any examinations or inspections being required for the whole period of their pregnancy and nursing.*
2. *If, however, such a woman found blood or a stain she becomes a "Niddah" in every respect. She should consult with a Rabbi concerning the possible recurrence of bleeding at her next period.*

3. *After the pregnancy is over and the child has been weaned, the mother may expect the return of her menses according to her former periods. (See above p. 163)*

4. *A pregnant or nursing woman who feels the opening of the womb or the emission of fluid, but on checking finds no trace of blood or stain does* not *become a "Niddah."*

5. *Childbirth causes the wife to be forbidden to her husband just as if she were a "Niddah." If she bears a son, she must count seven days of impurity after which, if the blood has stopped, she may make a "transition to purity" inspection, count seven days clear of blood, immerse herself in the Mikveh and thereafter resume relations with her husband in the normal way. If she bears a daughter, she must count fourteen days of impurity after which she makes a "transition to purity" inspection, counts seven days clear of blood, immerses herself in the Mikveh and then resumes relations with her husband in the normal way.*

MAIN LAWS CONCERNING THE BRIDE

1. *After the date of the wedding has been set, the bride should make a "transition to purity" inspection (preferably under the guidance of an experienced married woman), count seven days clear of blood and then immerse herself in the Mikveh. This applies to any bride, young and old,*

even if she no longer menstruates. No more than four days should intervene between the visit to the Mikveh and the marriage night.

2.   *A bride may immerse herself in the Mikveh during the day, but she must then immerse herself on the eighth day and not on the seventh unless there is some specially urgent necessity, in which case a competent Rabbi should be consulted.*

3.   *A bride the date of whose wedding is for some reason postponed after she has already made the "transition to purity" inspection, counted seven days clear of blood, immersed herself in the Mikveh, or while she is still counting the seven days, must consult a competent Rabbi as to the procedure to be followed.*

4.   *A bride who has not immersed herself in the Mikveh before the wedding, or who found blood after immersing herself in the Mikveh, is a Niddah, and may not remain completely alone with her bridegroom even during the day, until she counts the days of impurity, makes the "transition to impurity" examination, counts seven days clear of blood and immerses herself in the Mikveh.*

5.   *The blood of defloration counts as blood which makes the bride a Niddah. For this reason after their first relations with each other, if the bride is a virgin, the husband must separate himself from her, even if no blood is noticed. But whereas in normal cases, the Niddah counts five days of impurity, the bride counts only four days of impurity, and then makes the "transition to purity" examination and counts seven days clear of blood.*

6.   *If she finds blood after the "transition to purity" or after the immersion in the Mikveh, she must wait until the blood stops flowing, make the "transition to purity" again and then count seven days clear of blood and then immerse herself in the Mikveh.*

7.   *On the wedding night, the husband may complete the marital act with his virgin wife even though the blood (of virginity) is flowing. But immediately afterwards he must separate himself from her.*

SEPARATION

A woman for whom relations with her husband have been temporarily forbidden on account of menstrual bleeding or staining, remains forbidden even after having made the "transition to purity" inspection and counted seven days clear of blood and even after having washed herself thoroughly in a bathtub or shower. Only a ritual immersion in the Mikveh permits the resumption of marital relations.

The verse (Lev. 18, 19) says: "And thou shalt not approach unto a woman as long as she is impure by uncleanness." From which we understand that any sort of approaching is forbidden. The following are some of the things said by the Rabbis in connection with the separation of husband and wife until ritual immersion in the Mikveh: ·

They should not touch each other or pass things by hand to each other. They are not allowed to sleep in one bed even if both are fully dressed and each has a separate cover. They must abstain from any relations of affection. The husband should not look at his wife when she is undressed, nor should he be playful or lightheaded with her, either in deed or speech. When they eat alone at one table something unusual should be placed on the table in order to remind them to keep apart. The husband should not eat the left-overs of her food nor drink the left-overs of her drink unless these leftovers have first been poured into a different plate or utensil or unless a third person has eaten of them before him. He is not allowed to sleep or sit on her bed even when she is not present. His wife may not make his bed in his presence or sit on his bed in his presence.

If one of them is ill someone else should preferably attend to the sick person, but if no one else is available, it is customary for one to attend to the other's needs.

All these things apply after the wife has seen blood (or stains), but if she merely separates herself from him because her menstrual period is due on that day (see above) then these abstentions do not apply. However it is wiser for them to abstain from all relations with each other even in that case.

175

CHAPTER 22

■ CIRCUMCISION

■ "And when Abram was ninety years old and nine, the Lord appeared to Abram and said unto him: 'I am the God Almighty; walk before Me and be thou whole-hearted. And I will make My covenant between Me and thee, and thou shalt be the father of a multitude of nations. Neither shall thy name any more be called Abram, but thy name shall be Abraham; for the father of a multitude of nations have I made thee. And I will make thee exceedingly fruitful, and I will make nations of thee, and kings shall come out of thee. And I will establish My covenant between Me and thee, and thy seed after thee throughout their generations for an everlasting covenant, to be a God unto thee and thy seed after thee. And I will give unto thee and to thy seed after thee, the land of thy sojourning, all the land of Canaan, for an everlasting possession; and I will be your God.' And God said to Abraham: 'As for thee, thou shalt keep My covenant, thou and thy seed after thee throughout their generations. This is My covenant which ye shall keep between Me and you and thy seed after thee: every male among you shall be circumcised. And ye shall be circumcised in the flesh of your foreskin; and it shall be a token of a covenant betwixt me and you. And he that is eight days old shall be circumcised among you, every male throughout your generations . . . . And My covenant shall be in your flesh for an everlasting covenant. And the uncircumcised male who is not circumcised in the flesh of his foreskin, that soul shall be cut off from his people, he hath broken My covenant . . .' And God said: 'Nay, but Sarah thy wife shall bear thee a son; and thou shalt call his name Isaac; and I will establish My covenant with him for an everlasting covenant for his seed after him . . . But My covenant will I establish with Isaac' " (Genesis).

DIVINE MYSTERY IS REVEALED TO THE GOD-FEARING

"Why did God not give the mitzvah of circumcision (milah) to any one before Abraham? Scripture says: 'The secret of the Lord is with them that fear Him; and His covenant, to make them know it' (Psalms 25). What is 'the secret of the Lord'? It is the mitzvah of circumcision which He revealed to no one until twenty generations had passed from the time of Adam, and Abraham came and God passed that secret to him. God said to Abraham: 'If you are circumcised, you will take the secret.' [The Hebrew word for "you will be circumcised" is *timol*; the word for "you will take" is *titol*.] 'The secret of the Lord is with them that fear Him' — the Hebrew word for 'secret' [*sod*] has three letters, samech, vav, daleth, whose numerical value adds up to 70. I will establish 70 souls from you through the merit of circumcision . . . And for them I will establish 70 elders . . . And from them I will establish Moses, who will dwell in the Torah in 70 languages through the merit of circumcision" (Yalkut Shimoni Psalms).

The world was not worthy of the mitzvah of circumcision until Abraham was born. For Abraham's sake, God waited twenty generations until he would arrive, that He might reveal to him the secret mystery of circumcision with all its connotations: 70 souls of the children of Israel were to go down to Egypt, where their number was to be increased, by the time of their departure, to 600,000, the hosts of the Lord; 70 elders were to bear the burden of the whole people, and transform — by their wisdom — a mass of slaves in bondage to Pharaoh into a kingdom of priests and a holy people; our teacher Moses was to appear and teach his people Israel to disseminate the Torah's teaching among the 70 nations of the earth in 70 languages, that the earth may be filled with the knowledge of God at the end of days. All this greatness is reserved for Abraham and his children as reward for their performance of the mitzvah of circumcision in loyalty to His covenant. Hence it is said: "The secret of the Lord is with them that fear Him, and His covenant to make them know it."

THE MERIT OF CIRCUMCISION — THE EXISTENCE OF THE WORLD

If one serves God and does not enter a covenant with Him, it is possible that he serves himself. The nearness of God is a good thing for him, and he therefore serves God. He who serves God for his own good might be envious of others. Should they draw near to God like him, they would be in his eyes as detractors from his nearness to God; as if, Heaven forbid, God's powers were insufficient for all the world's inhabitants. If one serves God out of self-love, he serves as long as he derives benefit thereby; if not, he forsakes the worship of God, because he is not bound by a covenant. He is unworthy to lead others in the service of God, for if his followers should ever excel over him in the service of God, he would become angry with envy. Should he ever forsake his faith, all his followers might also forsake theirs. One who serves God however, under a covenant whose seal is indelibly stamped in his flesh — will serve his God for the sake of Heaven alone. One who enters a Divine covenant will not forsake his faith, and will not be envious of others. To the contrary, he will desire to share his faith with all, and to bring all others under the same wings of the Divine Presence which are his shelter. For he is a Ben Brith (son of a covenant); a covenant which stands between himself and God. Just as God desires to draw all the world's inhabitants near to Himself, similarly does he desire it. For God is sufficient (in His power and blessing) unto every creature. (See Rashi, Genesis 17:1.)

"God said to Abraham: 'From the time I created My world I waited twenty generations for you to come and accept the mitzvah of circumcision. If you will not accept it now, I shall return the world to chaos, for I no longer will have need of the world. If you do accept circumcision, the world will be worthy for Me and for you." (Yalkut Shimoni Genesis.)

God has no wish to sustain a world which acknowledges or denies Him, just as it sees fit. He desires a world whose inhabitants are sworn to him eternally, and who bear the indelible sign of

His covenant – a covenant which will endure despite all denials, one which all the world will recognize as the sign of the servants of God. However few their numbers, the world exists for their sake.

WITHOUT BLEMISH

"And you shall be whole-hearted" — Rabbi Judah the Prince says: 'Great in circumcision, for there was none so concerned with the practice of mitzvoth as our father Abraham, and he was called "whole-hearted" only because of the performance of the rite of circumcision.' For it is said in Scripture: 'Walk before Me and be whole-hearted' " (Nedarim 32).

One may perform all the mitzvoth, but if he does not bear on his body the sign of the covenant between himself and his God, he is not deemed whole-hearted. With that sign sealed in his flesh, he *is* whole-hearted.

Before he was circumcised Abraham controlled every part of his body in the service of his Creator — all but his eyes, ears, and organ of procreation. For a person sees, hears, and thinks involuntarily. When Abraham was consecrated through the covenant of circumcision, God gave him control over *all* of his body, that he might see, hear, and think only what his heart desired and that which was acceptable to the Lord. Therefore it is said in Scripture: "And you shall be 'whole-hearted' — wholly in control of all your body." (See Nedarim 32.)

THE WEAPON OF GOD

" 'And I will make My covenant between Me and thee.' — Once there was a king who had a dear friend who was very wealthy. The king said to his friend: 'What can I give you? You have much silver and much gold. I shall gird you with my weapons!' In the same way, God said to Abraham: 'What can I give you? You have silver and gold', as it said: 'And Abraham was very rich in cattle, in silver, and in gold.' It is sufficient for you to be like Me, as it is said: 'And I will make My covenant between Me and thee.' " (Midrash, cited by Rabbi Jacob Emden in Migdal Oz.)

If humanity rebels against God, He can always subdue them. His weapon is the covenant He made with Noah after the flood, that he would not again allow man to sink so deep into sin as to be beyond redemption. God promised to exact retribution from men

179

for their sins before the sins become intolerable. "Neither shall all flesh be cut off any more by the waters of the flood, neither shall there any more be a flood to destroy the earth."

Till Abraham came, God alone observed this covenant ensuring the world's survival. When the generation that built the tower of Babel sinned against Him, He exacted retribution from the wicked before they could cause the destruction of the entire earth. However, in those days the righteous men did not use God's weapon against the wicked — God acted alone. When Abraham came, God made him partner to His covenant with the world. Girding Abraham with his weapon of circumcision, God, so to speak, said to him: "Go forth and conquer My world in My name, that the world may endure."

A SOURCE OF STRENGTH

" 'And Abram fell on his face.' — Till he was circumcised, Abram had not the strength to stand when the Presence of God addressed him, and fell to the ground. After being circumcised, he had the strength to remain standing when God spoke with him. As it is said: 'But Abraham stood yet before the Lord.' More than this, God was revealed to him even while he was seated. As it is said: 'And the Lord appeared unto him by the terebinths of Mamre as he sat in the tent door.' " (Tanchuma Genesis 20.)

The Presence of God's glory appears to a man only when his spirit, soul and flesh have been purified and have submitted to the will of God. Such submission enables a person to stand upright. Before he was circumcised the spirit and soul of Abraham were already purified and submissive to God. But so long as his flesh was still uncircumcised, his eye, ear, and procreative organ remained each in its own domain. Upon them fear of God did not yet rest. The voice of God could stir the soul, but the flesh remained confused. After Abraham had circumcised his flesh and made it submissive to God's Majesty, his soul achieved dominion over all his limbs. From that hour his soul and body together, had the strength to stand in the presence of God. Their submission enabled them to stand upright.

Since the sign of the covenant in the flesh of the circumcised gives them the strength to stand upright, it also gives similar strength to the entire people of Israel in an hour of war against its enemies. 'For the Lord thy God walketh in the midst of thy camp, to deliver thee and to give up thine enemies before thee;

therefore shall thy camp be holy, that He see no unseemly thing in thee, and turn away from thee.' (Deut. 23.)

Similarly, when Joshua led the people of Israel across the waters of the Jordan, he did not begin the war to conquer the land till he had circumcised all those born in the wilderness, who were therefore still uncircumcised; in order that Israel should know that not by its sword would it gain possession of the land, but rather through the strength of God and the light of His countenance, through reaffirmation of the Divine covenant with Abraham.

"At that time the Lord said unto Joshua: 'Make thee knives of flint, and circumcise again the children of Israel the second time' (Joshua 5); so that they might be able to stand before their enemies."

" 'And I will give unto thee and to thy seed after thee, the land of thy sojourning, all the land of Canaan, for an everlasting possession, and I will be your God. And God said to Abraham: As for thee, thou shalt observe My covenant, thou and thy seed.' We learn from this that Israel was to inherit the land of Canaan from its forbears only through the merit of circumcision. On this condition was the land given to Abraham. And for this reason did God command Joshua to circumcise the people of Israel when they were about to enter into the land." (Midrash.)

"———Joshua said to them: 'Do you think that you will enter the land uncircumcised? Thus did God say to Abraham: and I will give to thee and to thy seed after thee the land of thy sojourning on condition that thou shalt observe My covenant.' " (Genesis Rabbah 46.)

HONOR RATHER THAN SHAME

"The Torah placed the covenant of circumcision where it did that the fear of God might be a preventive of sin." (Yalkut Deut.)

It was as a mark of His great love for Abraham and his children that God placed the seal of His name on an organ which has often been the source of sin and shame. In so doing, God sanctified man and purified him at the source of sin and shame.

The man whom fear of God restrains from the worst of sins, the man who overcomes the source of all sin and consecrates the root of all shame to God — that man has all his pleasures and actions under control. That man can emerge victorious over all evil, bringing it under subjection to the good.

SIGN OF THE COVENANT

Of all the 613 commandments in the Torah, only three were chosen to be "signs:" the Sabbath, Tephillin, and circumcision.

Of the Sabbath, the Torah says: "It is a sign between Me and the children of Israel for ever; for in six days the Lord made heaven and earth, and on the seventh day He ceased from work and rested." (Exodus 31.)

Of phylacteries it is said in the Torah: "And it shall be for a sign upon thy hand, and for frontlets between thine eyes, for by strength of hand the Lord brought us forth out of Egypt." (Ibid. 13.)

Of circumcision the Torah says: "And it shall be a sign of a covenant between Me and you." (Genesis 17.)

Three different signs, and three different testimonies.

The sign of the Sabbath testifies to the power of God, working in every action and in the act of creation. In observing the sign of the Sabbath we acknowledge that all our acts must be in consonance with the will of the Creator.

The sign of phylacteries testifies to God's power and providence in history. The nations of the earth are dependent on God's will alone for strength and weakness. Hence, the people of Israel place the sign of phylacteries on the left hand to acknowledge that it was God's arm, not theirs, that delivered them from Egypt.

The sign of the covenant of circumcision testifies to God's power over the processes of body and soul. For body and soul are not two separate and opposed areas: together they comprise one area, controlled by one Master. Man's thoughts and feelings all are rooted in one source. They are the creatures of God, and hymn His praise. Even more important: Paradoxically, the praise of God that issues from the darkness of the body and its desires is greater even than the heavenly praise that issues from the soul. And the covenant whose sign is sealed in man's body, signifying man's submission to the God who is exalted above all His creatures — that covenant and sign elevated man, making him worthy to aspire to so exalted a state.

REJOICING IN THE MITZVAH

"Said Rabbi Shimon the son of Yochai: 'Behold, a man loves nothing more than his own son, and yet circumcises him!'" Said Rabbi Nachman the son of Samuel: "He does so to do the will of his Maker." The father rejoices over the mitzvah, though he sees his son's blood being shed.

"Rabbi Chanina said: 'The father does even more than that — he goes to the expense of making the day of circumcision a day of rejoicing, a thing he was not commanded to do.'

"Even more: a person will borrow if necessary, in order to make that day a day of rejoicing." (Midrash Tanchumah.)

"Rabban Shimon the son of Gamaliel said: 'Every mitzvah which the people of Israel accepted with rejoicing, like circumcision . . . they still perform with rejoicing.'" (Sabbath 130.)

"From this you may learn that he who brings his son to be circumcised is likened to a High Priest placing his offerings on the altar. That is why they said: 'A person is obligated to make the day of his son's circumcision a day of festivity and happiness.'" (Yalkut Genesis.)

Why do we rejoice over this mitzvah?

Because it is a mark of the covenant between God and us, and it remains on us all of our lives.

THE PRECIOUSNESS OF THE MITZVAH

"Rabbi Yishmael said: 'Great is the mitzvah of Milah, for thirteen covenants were struck over it.'" (The term covenant is used thirteen times in the Biblical passage of Milah—see Nedarim 31.)

"And these thirteen covenants allude to the thirteen attributes of Divine mercy." (It is as reward for the mitzvah of Milah that God was revealed to Israel in all the attributes of His mercy.) (Rabbi Jacob Emden in Migdal Oz.)

"Rabbi Yose said: 'Great is the mitzvah of Milah for it takes precedence even over the severity of the Sabbath.'" (Nedarim ibid.)

"Great is the mitzvah of Milah for it is equal in importance to all the remaining mitzvoth of the Torah." (Ibid.)

"Great is the mitzvah of Milah for without it, Heaven and Earth could not endure." (Ibid.)

"Great is Milah for a child does not enter the count of the generations unless he be circumcised." (Midrash.)

"Even if the people of Israel should have no righteous deeds to their credit, God will redeem them through the merit of the mitzvah of Milah." (Agadath Bereshith 17.)

"If a person is not circumcised he is unable to study Torah. Akilas, the nephew of the Roman Emperor Hadrian, wanted to become converted to Judaism, but he feared his uncle Hadrian. He (Akilas) said to him (Hadrian): 'I want to do business, and to understand the thinking of people — and I want your advice.' Said he (Hadrian): 'Any type of business which you see as completely lowly unto earth – go and engage in it, because in the end its status will rise, and you will profit.' Akilas came to the land of Israel, he studied Torah and became a convert to Judaism. He then returned to his uncle. Hadrian said to him: 'Why is your face altered; it seems to me that your business venture failed, or perhaps some person has inflicted harm upon you.' Said Akilas to him: 'No, such a thing did not occur.' Said Hadrian to him: 'Why is your face altered?' Akilas replied: 'I studied Torah, and I also was circumcised.' Said he: 'And who advised you thus?' Whereupon Akilas replied: I sought your advice — and you said to me, any type of business which you see to be lowly unto earth, go and engage in it for in the end its status will rise" — I traversed all the lands, and nowhere did I see a people as lowly unto earth as Israel; in the end its status will rise.' Hadrian said to him: 'Will you not tell me why you did this thing?' He said: 'I wanted to study Torah.' Said Hadrian: 'You should have studied Torah and not been circumcised.' Said Akilas to him: 'Do you reveal your confidence to one who is not utterly devoted to you unto death? Similarly, if a person is not circumcised he is incapable of studying Torah.'" (Midrash.)

THE OBSERVANCE OF BRITH MILAH

CUSTOMS BEFORE THE BRITH

1. *It is customary for school children to be brought to the room of the new-born baby, every day till the day of the Brith; The children read the first passage of the Shema and they are given sweets.*
2. *On the eve of the Sabbath which precedes the Brith, it is customary to hold a 'Shalom Zachar' celebration in honor of the new-born child, after the Sabbath meal. Refreshments are served, there is singing, and the Shema is recited (if the gathering takes place where the baby is).*
3. *It is customary in most places to stay awake the last night before the Brith; Torah is studied, and a moderately festive meal is served.*

ESSENTIAL LAWS AND CUSTOMS OF CIRCUMCISION

1. *It is a positive commandment of the Torah that a father is to circumcise his son on the eighth day after the child's birth.*

2. *If a father does not circumcise his son, the Beth Din (literally, Rabbinic Tribunal, which represents the community) is obligated to circumcise the child.*

3. *If the Beth Din does not have him circumcised, he is obligated to see to his own circumcision when he reaches adulthood. If he fails to do so, he is subject to the Divinely imposed the penalty of kareth (excision of the soul); which penalty rests upon him constantly for as long as he delays his circumcision.*

4. *If the father knows how to perform the act of circumcision, he circumcises his son himself. If he lacks such knowledge, he designates the mohel as a delegate to perform the Mitzvah in his behalf.*

5. *If the father designates one mohel to circumcise his son, he may not chage his mind and bring another one. But if the second mohel is more God-fearing or technically more competent than the first, the father may change his mind, in order to perform the mitzvah in the best possible manner.*

6. *A person should seek after a mohel who is God fearing and upright in his ways. The mohel must however possess unquestioned technical competence.*

7. *If a child is ill, the Brith is delayed till he regains health, and an additional seven days have passed thereafter. All depends on the advice of the doctor and the mohel. It is necessary to exercise utmost care in these matters. If there is any suspicion of illness, circumcision should not be performed, for danger to life takes precedence over all else. It is possible to perform circumcision later, but it is not possible to restore a life.*

8. *The Brith is properly performed during the entire eighth day — from sunrise to sunset. However, "the diligent perform a mitzvah as early as possible" and they perform the Brith during the morning hours. If there was delay, and the Brith did not take place till sunset, circumcision may still take place, in the last resort, during the twilight period before the appearance of the stars.*

9. *If a child was born during the twlight period of the day, the eight day count is begun from the night. If however, the eighth day in such a case, falls on Sabbath or Yom Tov, the Brith is delayed another day. If, in the given instance, the eighth day falls on a Sabbath or a holiday, which is succeeded by another Sabbath or festival day, then the Brith is delayed two dqys. If, in such an instance, the eighth day falls on a Thursday which is also the first day of Rosh Hashannah, then the Brith is delayed three days till after the Sabbath.*

10. *Outside the land of Israel, in such an instance (if the eighth day falls on a Thursday which is also the first day of any holiday other than Rosh Hashannah), then the Brith is only delayed till the second day of Yom Tov.*

11.   *It is customary to prepare an ornate chair to serve as "the chair of Elijah, the Angel of the Covenant." The child is placed on the chair before the Brith, and is circumcised on it. The father or the Mohel designates the chair verbally, and says 'this is the chair of Elijah, the Angel of the Covenant, who is remembered for good.'*

12.   *Because of the preciousness of the mitzvah it is customary to assign its various parts to separate persons. The following is a list of the customary honors:*

(a) A married or engaged couple is assigned the task of bringing the infant from the mother to the "place of the mitzvah." The wife, or the bride, takes the infant and brings it to the men's section in the Synagogue, (if the Brith is performed in a home — to the room in which the Brith is to take place). The husband, or groom, then takes the child from her hand and brings it to the "place of the mitzvah."

(b) "The Chair of Elijah" — a designated person takes the child from the one who previously held it and places it on the "Chair of Elijah."

(c) The next honoree takes the infant from the chair, holds it in his arms briefly, and hands the child over to the sandek (to be explained in d). This part of the mitzvah may be given to a number of people, one after the other.

(d) "sandek" — the designaton of the one who holds the infant on his knees during the circumcision. It is the most important of the honors and is assigned to one who is upright and God-fearing. The sandek should purify himself, and wear festive clothing, for the day is as a holiday to him. The sandek, the father of the child and the mohel should take hair cuts and dress well in honor of the day. Since the task assigned to the sandek is such an honored one, it is customary not to assign it to one person for two brothers. It is customary for the sandek to make a gift to the circumcised infant. He also shares the expense of the Brith with the father.

(e) "mohel" — The one who circumcises the infant.

187

(f) The person assigned to recite the prescribed blessings after the Brith.

13.   *Some earth and sand are prepared in a dish, in which to place the severed foreskin. This is done in remembrance of the Divine promise: "And I shall make your seed as the dust of the earth and the sand of the sea." If the Brith takes place on Sabbath, the earth should be prepared before Sabbath.*

14.   *It is the custom of some to light candles at the time of the Brith in remembrance of: "Unto the Jews there was light and happiness and rejoicing." "Rejoicing" refers to the act of circumcision, as it is said: "I rejoice over Your command" (Psalms 119).*

15.   *If possible the mitzvah should be performed in the presence of ten Jewish persons.*

16.   *When the infant is brought to the circumcision room, all assembled rise and say: "Blessed is he who comes!" they remain standing until the end of the mitzvah.*

17.   *Before the Brith the mohel reads in a loud voice — and all present recite with him — the words of the verse: "Happy is he whom You choose and draw near, he shall dwell in Your courtyards, may we be sated by the goodness of Your house, the holiness of Your temple" (Psalms 65(.*

18.   *The mohel recites the first Blessing: "Blessed art Thou o Lord our God, King of the Universe, who sanctified us with His commandments and commanded us concerning circumcision." He severs the foreskin. After the foreskin is severed but before the membrane covering the milah is torn, the father of the child says: "Blessed art Thou o Lord our God, King of the Universe, who sanctified us with His commandments and commanded us to enter him (the child) into the covenant of Abraham our father." The mohel then rends the membrane and draws out the blood. In the lana of Israel it is customary for the father of the child to recite a second blessing at that moment: "Blessed art Thou o Lord our God, King of the Universe, who kept us alive, sustained us and brought to this time." All assembled answer Amen after each blessing. When the father finishes the recitation*

of his blessing all present respond in the following words: "Just as he entered the covenant, so may he enter into the Torah, the wedding canopy and good deeds." Some practise the custom of taking a myrtle branch in hand and reciting the blessing, "Who creates fragrant trees," after the circumcision blessings.

19. After the circumcision, the person designated to recite the blessings takes a cup of wine and recites the blessing over wine. He then recites a final blessing of praise and petition, which alludes to the child's consecration to God through the mark of the covenant, and voices the prayer that the merit of the covenant may ever lead to the deliverance of Israel. The name of the child is then announced and the following prayer is recited:

"Our God and the God of our fathers, sustain this child unto his father and his mother, and may his name be called in Israel .... the son of .... May his father rejoice in the one who comes out of his loins, and may his mother rejoice in the fruit of her womb. As it is written: 'May your father and your mother rejoice, and may she who gave birth to you be happy.' And it is said: 'And I passed over you and I saw you .... in your blood, and I said to you, by your blood you shall live (the mohel puts a drop of wine into the mouth of the infant) and I said to you, by your blood you shall live.' And it is said: 'He remembered His covenant unto eternity, the word which He commanded unto a thousand generations, which He covenanted with Abraham, and His oath to Isaac, which He established unto Jacob as a statute, unto Israel as an eternal covenant.' And it is said: 'And Abraham circumcised Isaac his son, at the age of eight days, as God commanded him.' 'Give thanks to the Lord for He is good, for unto eternity is His loving kindness.' This little one (the child's name is here inserted) will grow large. Just as he entered the covenant, so may he enter into the Torah, the wedding canopy, and the practice of good deeds."

20. Afterwards, a festive meal is tendered for the assembled, and the meal is considered as a "meal of mitzvah" (a meal which accompanies the fulfillment of a mitzvah, is in itself a mitzvah). It is customary that one invites, to a

Brith meal, only such persons as are likely to come. If the host knows however, that his invited guest will not come, he should not invite him, for one who refrains from participating in a meal given in observance of a mitzvah, is subject to Divine disfavor.

21.   *In the grace after meals several petitions are added at the appropriate place, in which Divine blessing is asked for the parents of the child, the newly circumcised infant, the mohel; and the coming of the Messiah and of Elijah is invoked.*

NAMING OF A DAUGHTER

It is customary to name a newborn daughter on the first Sabbath after the child's birth. The father comes to the Synagogue, he ascends to the Torah, the cantor or reader recites the prescribed blessing for the mother and the child "who was born to her, for good fortune and may her name be called in Israel ...."

Some name a baby daughter on the first Monday or Thursday after the child's birth, since on those days the Torah is read at the Synagogue.

Others delay the naming of a baby daughter till the child is thirty days old. It is proper for everyone to do in accord with the custom of his fathers.

It is praiseworthy to give a baby daughter a Biblical name.

THE BLESSING OF 'HAGOMEL' AFTER BIRTH

After the mother returns to her health, she comes to the Synagogue on Sabbath. On that Sabbath her husband ascends to the Torah and after he has completed his final blessing over the Torah, the mother recites, at her seat in the women's section: "Blessed art Thou o Lord our God, King of the Universe, who bestows goodness upon such as are liable, for having bestowed every goodness upon me." Her friends in the women's section respond after her: "Amen, He who has bestowed goodness upon you, shall bestow all that is good upon you forever."

It is the custom of some that the mother does not come

to the Synagogue till forty days have elapsed after the birth of a male child, or eighty days after the birth of a female child. It is customary with others, that, on the first Saturday night after the Brith, a minyon (quorum of 10) of men comes to the mother's home and recites the evening prayer there. After the evening prayer the mother recites the "Hagomel" blessing and all assembled answer Amen. With still others, it is customary for the mother to recite this blessing at the time of the Brith, in the event of the birth of a male child.

■ CHAPTER 23

■ THE REDEMPTION OF THE FIRST-BORN SON

(*Pidyon Ha-Ben*)

■ "And the Lord spoke unto Moses, saying: 'Sanctify unto Me all the first-born, whatsoever openeth the womb among the children of Israel, both of man and of beast, it is Mine . . . . And it came to pass, when Pharaoh would hardly let us go, that the Lord slew all the first-born in the land of Egypt, both the first-born of man, and the first-born of beast; therefore I sacrifice to the Lord all that openeth the womb, being males; but all the first-born of my sons I redeem.'" (Exodus 13, 1-15.)

"And the Lord spoke unto Moses, saying: 'And I, behold, I have taken the Levites from among the children of Israel instead of every first-born that openeth the womb among the children of Israel; and the Levites shall be Mine; for all the first-born are Mine; on the day that I smote all the first-born in the land of Egypt I hallowed unto Me all the first-born in Israel, both man and beast, Mine shall they be; I am the Lord.'" (Numbers 3, 11-13.)

"And the Lord spoke unto Moses, saying: 'Take the Levites instead of all the first-born among the children of Israel, and the cattle of the Levites instead of their cattle, and the Levites shall be Mine, even the Lord's. And as for the redemption of the two hundred and threescore and thirteen of the first-born of the children of Israel, that are over and above the number of the Levites, thou shalt take five shekels apiece by the poll; after the shekel of the sanctuary shalt thou take them — the shekel is twenty gerahs. And thou shalt give the money wherewith they that remain over of them are redeemed unto Aaron and to his sons.' " (Numbers 3, 44-48).

THE FIRST KOHANIM

Our rabbis said: "The Lord commanded that the first-born sons of the children of Israel should be redeemed by the Levites because originally the first-born males were dedicated to the service of God. Before the sanctuary was built, sacrifices could be made anywhere, and the rituals were performed by the first-born males. It was they who offered the sacrifices when Moses ascended mount Sinai. But when the children of Israel fashioned the golden calf, the first-born were also the ones who performed the ritual of the worship of the calf. Therefore the Lord said: 'I elevated the first-born, but they have turned against Me. So now I shall take the priesthood away from them and give it to the tribe of Levi, who took no part in the worship of the golden calf.' " (Bamidbar Rabbah 4.)

EVERY FIRST THING BELONGS TO GOD

Every first thing and the first-born of every creature belongs to God. David went still further, saying: "The earth is the Lord's, and the fullness thereof" (Psalms 24) — from which it would appear that all things, not merely all first things, belong to God. However, the Lord does not demand that we give Him all. He is content with first things and the first-born of all things.

That is why the children of Israel set aside the first-fruits of their produce and the first-born of their cattle, consecrating them to the Creator who made and gave them all. And we are permitted to enjoy the remainder only after having uttered the appropriate blessing. As our rabbis said: "Whosoever derives a benefit from the things of this world without uttering the appropriate blessing is deriving a benefit from things that belong to God, as it is said in Scripture: 'The earth is the Lord's and the fullness thereof.' " (Berachot 35.)

193

All the first fruits of the earth belong to God as it is written: "The choicest first-fruits of thy land thou shalt bring into the house of the Lord thy God." (Exodus 23.)

"The first-fruits of thy corn, of thy wine, and of thy oil, and the first of the fleece of thy sheep, thou shalt give Him" (Deut. 18). "... ye shall bring the sheaf of the first-fruits of your harvest unto the priest." (Leviticus 23.)

"Of the first of your dough ye shall give unto the Lord, a portion for a gift throughout your generations." (Numbers 15.)

"All the best of the oil, and all the best of the wine, and of the corn, the first part of them which they give unto the Lord, to thee (the Kohen) I have given them. The first-ripe fruits of all that is in their land, which they bring unto the Lord, shall be thine." (Numbers 18.)

All the first-born of the cattle and the sheep belong to God, as it is written:

"Howbeit the firstling among beasts, which is born as a firstling to the Lord ... it is the Lord's." (Leviticus 27.)

"All the firstling males unto the Lord thy God; thou shalt do no work with the firstling of thy flock." (Deut. 15.)

The first-fruits of the human womb also belong to God, as it is written: "Sanctify unto Me all the first-born, whatsoever openeth the womb among the children of Israel, both of man and of beast, it is Mine." (Exodus 22.)

The Torah itself is called the "firstling" and is God's, as it is written: "The Lord made me as the beginning of His way, the first of His works of old." (Proverbs 8.)

The first and beginning of all wisdom and of all understanding belongs to God, as it is said:

"The fear of the Lord is the beginning of wisdom." (Psalms 111.)

"The fear of the Lord is the beginning of knowledge." (Proverbs 1.)

The people of Israel is called a firstling, and belongs to God, as it is said in Scripture: "... the first of the nations." (Amos 6.)

"Israel is the Lord's hallowed portion, His first-fruits of the increase: all that devour Him shall be held guilty, evil shall come upon them." (Jeremiah 2.)

"And thou shalt say unto Pharaoh: Thus saith the Lord: Israel is My son, My first-born. And I have said unto thee: Let My son go, that he may serve Me; and thou hast refused to let him go. Behold, I will slay thy son, thy first-born." (Exodus 4.)

Pharaoh and all his people rejected God, Pharaoh saying, "Who is God that I should listen to Him." Therefore: "The Lord smote all the first-born in the land of Egypt, from the first-born of Pharaoh that sat on his throne unto the first-born of the captive that was in the dungeon; and all the first-born of cattle." (Exodus 12.)

But Israel believed in God; "And the people believed" (Exodus 4); "and they believed in the Lord and in His servant Moses" (Exodus 14). Thus believing, they entered into a covenant of blood with Him, the blood of circumcision and the blood of the paschal lamb. For this reason God passed over the houses of the children of Israel when He smote the Egyptians. It was not only the firstlings Israel gave to God; the entire people, from the oldest to the youngest, entered the covenant as one and became God's.

But though all Israel entered into the covenant with God, He singled out the firstling for dedication to His service: "Sanctify unto Me all the first-born . . . for all the first-born are Mine."

Our forefather Jacob, who took the birthright from his elder twin Esau, did so only because he so highly valued the sanctity attached to being a firstborn, which Esau would have desecrated — and also in order to gain the right to serve God, like a priest who offers sacrifices.

All the first-born sons of Israel, then, were singled out to worship and serve God, performing this service in the name of their brethren.

THE REDEMPTION IN EGYPT

The redemption of the first-born sons of the children of Israel in Egypt did not discharge them from God's service. Rather, it was intended to enable them to devote themselves to their own affairs — without, however, desecration of any sacred thing. Even after they were redeemed, they remained sacred. They were the ones who were to stand before God and worship Him. When the first-born served as priests, offering sacrifices to the golden calf, they disqualified themselves from continuing as Kohanim. Yet, though disqualified from the priesthood, the first-born remained holy, as the "first issue of the womb." Their special sanctity can only be removed by their redemption.

THE KOHEN AS THE SURROGATE OF THE FIRST-BORN

The first-born son must give a sum equivalent to the value of his service (five shekels, according to Scripture) to the Kohen, who is the elite of the tribe of Levi. By this act he relieves himself of the sanctity with which he was born — the Levite assuming it. The sanctity is not nullified — it is transferred through the redemption money given to the Kohen. Thus, the daily service of God still belongs, so to speak, to the first-born, who has merely transferred it to the Levite.

Though a father, in redeeming his first-born son, gives only the redemption money to the Kohen, he is considered to have dedicated his son entirely to Heaven: as Scripture says: "The first-born of thy sons shalt thou give unto Me." (Exodus 22.)

■ LAWS AND CUSTOMS CONCERNING THE REDEMPION OF THE FIRST-BORN SON (PIDYON HA-BEN)

1. *Every father is commanded by the Torah to redeem his first-born son thirty days after birth. The redemption-ceremony should take place on the thirty-first day and should not be delayed, unless the thirty-first day fell on Sabbath or a festival in which case one should wait till the morning after the Sabbath or festival.*

2. *The father may redeem his son wherever he may be, even though the son is not present.*

3. *If the father did not redeem him at the appointed time, he must redeem him afterwards.*

4. *If the father did not redeem him at all, the son must redeem himself when he grows up.*

5. *Only a first-born son of the mother must be redeemed. Thus a son who is the first-born to his father but not to his mother (i.e. where she had children from a previous marriage), need not be redeemed. If the mother had a miscarriage before giving birth to her first-born, a competent Rabbi should be consulted.*

6. *A first-born son born of a caesarian birth need not be redeemed.*

7. *If the father or mother are Kohen or Levite the first-born son need not be redeemed.*

8. *In the case of twins, where there is a boy and a girl, if the boy is born first, he must be redeemed; if the girl is born first then the boy need not be redeemed.*

9. *Even where the son has not yet been circumcised (e.g. for reasons of ill-health) his redemption should take place on the thirty-first day and should not be delayed.*

10. *The money with which the first-born is to be redeemed must be the equivalent of the five shekalim mentioned in the Torah. A competent Rabbi should be approached to determine the equivalent in local currency of the five shekalim mentioned in the Torah.*

11. *The father may redeem his son with either currency or goods to the value of five shekalim, as mentioned before, but he may not redeem him with bills or checks. If he attempted to redeem him with bills or checks, the redemption is invalid and a proper redemption must be made.*

12. *The Kohen who received the money or goods paid to redeem a first-born son, may return this money or goods as a present to the father if he wishes, but he need not do so. And in no case may the father give him the money or goods on condition that he return them.*

13. *Every Kohen is permitted to receive the money or goods and thereby redeem the first-born son. However it is customary to seek out for this purpose, a Kohen who is a Talmudic scholar and whose priestly ancestry is certain.*

14. *The father may divide the money (or goods) among several Kohanim, each one receiving only a part of the total sum involved, and redeem his child in this way.*

15. *If a father promised a particular Kohen that he would give him the money in order to redeem his son, he may not change his mind and bring another Kohen.*

THE CEREMONY

1. *One dresses the child in its best clothes, and the father brings him before the Kohen. He places the money (or goods) equivalent to five shekalim before the Kohen and says, "My wife, who is like myself an Israelite (and not a Kohen or Levite), has born me this first-born son and I hereby give him to you."*

2. *The Kohen replies: "What do you prefer, your first-born son or the five shekalim which you are obliged to give me in order to redeem him?"*

3. *The father says: "I want my first-born son, and here is the money for redeeming him, as I am obliged to give."*

4. *While handing over the money to the Kohen and before the Kohen receives it, the father recites the two blessings which follow:*

"Blessed art Thou, o Lord our God, King of the Universe Who hath sanctified us with His Commandments and commanded us concerning the redemption of the first-born son."

"Blessed art Thou, o Lord our God, King of the Universe Who hath given us life, and preserved us, and enabled us to reach this event."

5. *After completing the blessings, the father gives the money to the Kohen and the Kohen takes a glass of wine and recites over it the appropriate blessing. It is also customary, in some lands, to prepare fragrant myrtle leaves which the Kohen smells, reciting the appropriate blessing.*

6. *The Kohen then takes the money, and, holding it over the head of the child, he says: "This is instead of that, this is in exchange of that, this is in remission of that. May this child live, may he learn Torah, and may the fear of Heaven be upon him. May it be God's will that even as he has been admitted to redemption, so may he enter the gates of Torah, the marriage canopy, and a life of good deeds. Amen." The Kohen then places his hand upon the head of the child, and blesses him as follows:*

"May the Lord make thee as Ephraim and Manasseh. May He Bless thee and keep thee; may the Lord turn His face unto thee, and give thee peace.

The Lord is thy guardian; the Lord is thy shadow upon thy right hand. For length of days, and years of life and peace shall they add to thee. The Lord shall guard thee from all evil; He shall guard thy soul."

7. *The entire ceremony precedes a festive meal in honor of the occasion. However, the act of washing the hands and the breaking of bread precede the ceremony.*

CHAPTER 24

■ BRINGING UP CHILDREN

■ Of all the activities in which a person is engaged, none is more praiseworthy than proper upbringing of one's sons and daughters. If a person has refrained from committing a wrong, it is as if he had performed a mitzvah. If one performs mitzvoth his reward is assured in this world and in the next. If one causes others to perform mitzvoth, the merit of the many adheres to him. If he studies Torah and teaches it to others; if he illuminates his own life as well as the life of others, through the practice of mitzvoth, till all the world is inclined to the scale of merit — there is none more righteous than he. For he is beloved by God and man. However, there is one whom God loves even more — a person who devotes his utmost strength to the proper upbringing of his sons and daughters. Thus, we find that Abraham was praised for bringing up his children more than for any other deed. It is said concerning Abraham: 'For I have known him in order that he may instruct his sons and his household after him, that they may keep the way of the Lord to do righteousness and justice, in order that the Lord may bring upon Abraham all that He spoke concerning him.' (Genesis 18.) Abraham was praised for the upbringing of his children more than for all his other deeds.

GOD DESIRES LIFE FOR HIS CREATURES

Abraham fed all comers to his home and bestowed kindness upon many. He proclaimed the Name of the Lord, the Eternal God, and taught people truth and knowledge. Abraham waged war against idolatry and the abomination associated with its practice; for the idolators of old offered even their sons and daughters as altar sacrifices. Abraham walked wholeheartedly before his God and did not doubt His justice. For His sake Abraham allowed himself to be cast into a burning furnace, and for His sake he brought up his only son for an altar offering. Our father Abraham was tried by ten tests (of faith), and he prevailed against them all. However the test of the binding of Isaac was the severest of all to him. Not only because of his love for his son, but for another reason, which burdened Abraham greatly. He had proclaimed to all: 'God does not desire human sacrifices, they are an abomination!' Now he has to bring up his son as an altar offering. If people would ask him: 'Where is your son?' — what could he say to them? Nevertheless he did not doubt God's justice. And he said: 'I will walk before God even if He takes away all that I have, and gives me nothing.' From east to west, from north to south, the righteousness of our father Abraham shines. As for himself — he is childless and the overseer of his house will inherit him. God appeared to him and said: 'Look now heavenward and count the stars, can you count them? — thus shall your seed be.' And Abraham 'trusted unto the Lord and he considered it unto Him as righteousness.' That is to say, he believed that God bestows undeserved gifts upon His creatures, in His righteousness. He felt however, that he himself did not deserve the gift promised him.

We see from this how profound Abraham's faith and humility were. God Himself however, ascribes His special relationship to Abraham to the latter's upbringing of his children alone. 'For I have known him in order that he should instruct his sons and household after him.'

All the practice of righteousness and performance of good deeds that a person might be engaged in all the days of his life, are not as valued as the righteousness he practices in properly upbringing his own sons and daughters 'that they might observe the way of the Lord to do righteousness and justice.'

Why is this so? For God desires life for all His creatures. When He created His world, He created it to endure eternally. Therefore, the mitzvah of 'and he shall live by them,' suspends all other commandments. For, the life of Israel is more beloved by God than the practice of a mitzvah (Rashi Yoma 82). The world was created and the Torah was given for the living and not for the dead. Even after the first sin which brought death into the world (an end which no one escapes), no man dies a complete death. Rather does he remain alive in his children. But this is so only if the life of children is a continuation of the ways of their parents. If the children depart from the ways of their parents, then their parents are dead. And even if a person causes others, who are not his children, to adhere to his ways, he is not as much alive in them after his death as he would be in his children. In the end those others are likely to depart from his ways entirely. Of all the people converted to monotheism by Abraham and Sarah in Charan and Kasdim, in Aram-Naharaim and Egypt, none remained faithful to God. Abraham's teachings lived on only in Isaac, Jacob and their descendants.

All the same, a person to whom God denies children, but who practices mitzvoth and good deeds; who sustains the Divine covenant, and strives to teach Torah to the children of others — is accounted by Scripture as possessed of eternal life. Of such as him was it said: 'And I will give them in my house and in my walls a hand and name better than sons and daughters; an eternal name wil lI give him which will not be cut off' (Isaiah 56). Similarly did the Rabbis say: 'If one teaches Torah to the son of his fellow, will I give him which will not be cut off' (Isaiah 56). Similarly did (Sanhedrin 19).

Therefore, a person who acquires a treasure of mitzvoth and good deeds, achieves the merit they bestow. If one causes others to do the same, the merit of the many is his. But if one guides his sons and daughters on the way to truth — he gives life to himself and to them; and the mitzvah of life is greater than all the other mitzvoth, for it is said: 'And he shall live by them.'

TWO OPEN BOOKS

The mitzvah of the upbringing of children is exceedingly great, for it applies to men and women, to adults and children, to little ones and infants, and even to newborn babies and sucklings.

When a person is born, two books are immediately opened before him: the book of life and the book of education.

Adults enter the house of study,, they study Torah, and acquire knowledge from their teachers. Children come to their teacher to be taught Torah, Prophets and Writings, and to be trained in the practice of mitzvoth. Infants are brought by their fathers and mothers to the "hallway of Torah," and they are taught "Aleph-Beth," and "Moses instructed us in Torah as an inheritance." They are taught blessings, and "Hear O Israel." But, even newborn babies and sucklings are also "given upbringing."

Just as the book of life is opened for a new-born child at the beginning of his life, similarly is the book of education then opened to him.

What is the title of the first chapter in the book of a baby's life? — "the drawing of nourishment."

The child does not strive, nor work, for he is still too weak for the labors which are to be his future tasks. All the same, he is already a person, for he already eats the fruit of his first deed; a deed which sustains his life. What is his first deed? — the drawing of nourishment from his mother. His food no longer comes to him of itself. He needs to draw nourishment in order to live. For this is the entire life of man; to strive is man born.

What name shall we give to the first "book of education?" Let us call it: "The chapter of overflowing love." Who teaches the first chapter? — the mother. As we have said previously: the beginning of all good comes from the mother. A child's education is begun by his mother. The mother who bore the child is the first to educate him, and the first lesson she teaches him is that of love.

AN OVERFLOWING LOVE

This is the secret of education. When a person begins to strive, immediately an overflowing of blessing is opened for him. His striving is not for nought. When a person turns to his source and seeks to draw nourishment from his own well-spring, the latter opens for him and yields all its treasures to him. He seeks nourishment for the hour, but obtains nourishment also for the remainder of all his days. Such is the nourishment which a mother's love gives to her children. And in all the world, no love is greater.

As long as the child is still within the body of his mother he is flesh of her flesh, and limb of her limbs. And she is fashioned in such a manner that her baby's needs are fulfilled naturally, without conscious attention. When the baby emerges into the world, he becomes a new person, an individual unto himself. But as a person he is still small, weak and lacking. What a long way he is to traverse! It is time to begin his upbringing and education. And there is no introduction to the "book of education" other than that of love.

FROM MOTHER TO TEACHER

The Jewish mother gives all the wealth of her heart to her child. Her noblest dreams are dreamt for her child. Her thoughts during the day and night are given to him. Her trembling and all the intensity of her yearning are for the one born to her. Upon him her eyes are cast from evening to morning. And she dwells constantly in thoughts of love for him. It is this ocean of love in whose waters the infant is immersed and purified every hour, to prepare him for a future life of purity.

The Jewish mother has a great wealth of love; for her natural mother-love is enlarged by the flow of love which comes from her sacred inheritance — a love for what is most exalted under the heavens.

After the Jewish mother has wrapped up all the goodness of the earth and given it to her child, she is not yet satisfied. All the expanses of the heavens, all the light in them — till the light of the "Throne of Glory" — does she wish to give to her child. What is exalted beyond human understanding, is revealed and known to her. The worlds above are greatly beloved to her, and her child is greatly beloved to her — let her loved one possess all else that she loves.

Length of days and wealth, are not sufficient for her child. Glory and majesty — are not sufficient. "Let angels from above descend from the heavens to hear Torah from your mouth, my child; for its worth is greater than all commodities."

Jewish children did not always draw the beauty and grace of their childhood from the rays of the sun. For during the many generations which Israel spent in exile, Jewish children saw little of the light of the sun and beauty of nature. Most of their days were spent in the imprisonment of dark exile. Where then did they draw their beauty and grace, their cleverness and breadth of understanding? From the love of mother, from the rays of the angels who sought fragrance in listening to the Jewish mother's whispering, from the songs she sang to her child as he lay in his crib. Indeed, the period of the crib was, for Jewish children, nothing other than the hallway to the house of the teacher.

> "Behind the crib of my gentle child
> there stands a kid white and clean;
> the kid will go to ply commerce
> and my son will run to study Torah . . . ."

or

> "Run my son, run hard
> and enter the house of your teacher, again and again
> search and seek only in the Torah
> for her wealth is better than all commodities . . . ."

These and similar songs were the lullabys with which the Jewish mother put her child to sleep. To sleep? — No! To awaken his still slumbering soul, to engrave in his heart the words of her Torah in letters of love pure as a flame of fire.

HEAR O ISRAEL

When a child is born, its parents immediately consecrate it to a life of Torah. Even before the infant understands what he hears, before he learns speech; even before his entry into the covenant of Abraham; from the earliest hours of his life his ears are habituated to listen to "Hear o Israel" from the mouths of slightly older friends of his. For it is customary wherever Jews live, that school children come to the home of a new-born baby, on each of the seven days between the baby's birth and the act of circumcision. There they read aloud the first passage of the Shema. "Hear O Israel, the Lord our God, the Lord is one!" Hear, o little Israel . . . . and you shall love the Lord your God———. And little Israel hears. For, when this child of Israel will grow up he will be unable to uproot the Torah from himself, even if he should subsequently seek to do so consciously. These words which he heard or which his fathers heard echo and re-echo in his ears. They bubble and emerge. And in the end all their strength and force will be revealed either in him, or in his son, or in his grandson.

MOTHER'S PRAYER — THE PRAYER OF THE HOUSE OF ISRAEL

Hannah, the wife of Elkanah, prayed all her days to God for a son. After her son Samuel was born to her, it is related of her: "And she nursed her son till she weaned him and she brought him up with her — and she brought him to the House of the Lord to Shiloh, and she said: "For this youth have I prayed and the Lord has granted my petition which I requested of Him, and I also have lent him to the Lord all the days" (Samuel 1:1).

Hannah's prayer when she "loaned" her son to the Lord, is the source of the laws of prayer and the order of prayer for the people of Israel through all the generations. Hannah's prayer, is the prayer of the entire congregation of Israel. For the Congregation of Israel has no greater prayer than that of Hannah, the prayer of a mother absorbed in the love of her son, and handing him over to the life of Torah.

This prayer of Hannah's, is the prophetic passage read on the New Year — the Day of Judgment — by all Israel, at the conclusion of the Torah reading. For the world has no better plea in the presence of the Divine Judge than its yearning to raise children for a life of righteousness and justice. Were it not for this, the whole world would return to chaos. The education and upbringing given to youth, sustains the world.

" 'Rabbi Joshua the son of Chananya — happy is she who gave birth to him' (Ethics of the Fathers 2). For his mother used to bring his cradle to the House of Study so that his ears might absorb words of Torah from the time when he lay in the cradle."

" 'Thus shall you say to the house of Jacob' — these are the women; 'and you shall tell the children of Israel' — these are the men. Why were the women to be told first? Because they are more diligent in the practice of mitzvoth; another reason is, that they might lead their children to the study of Torah" (Exodus Rabbah 28).

THE MOTHER OF THE CHILDREN

If you wish to know how great the strength of a mother can be in the upbringing of her children, you may do so from the words which Hannah, the mother of the seven sons, sent to Abraham our father in the true world, by the hand of her last son.

"———They brought the first one before the King, and said to him: 'Worship idols!' Said he to them: 'It is written in the Torah: I Am the Lord your God!' They took him out to be killed and brought the second. They said to him: 'Worship idols!' He replied: 'It is written in the Torah: thou shalt have no other gods before me!' They took him out to be killed and brought in the third son. They said to him: 'Worship idols!' Said he: 'It is written in the Torah: whoever slaughters sacrifices to idols shall be destroyed!' They put him to death. They brought the fourth and said to him: 'Worship idols!' Said he: 'It is written in the Torah: you shall not bow down to a strange god!' They took him and put him to

205

death. They brought the fifth one and said to him: 'Worship idols!' Said he: 'It is written in the Torah: Hear O Israel, the Lord our God, the Lord is One.' They took him out to be killed. They brought the sixth son and said to him: 'Worship idols!' Said he: 'It is written in the Torah: and you shall know this day and put it unto your heart that the Lord, He is God in the heavens above and on the earth below, there is none else!' They took him out, put him to death, and brought in the last one. They said to him: 'Worship idols!' Said he to them: 'It is written in the Torah: you have chosen the Lord — and the Lord hath chosen you this day. We are sworn to God that we will not exchange Him for any other god, and he has sworn to us that He will not exchange us for any other people!' Whereupon the king said: 'I will throw my ring on the floor; you need only bow down and pick it up, so that others might say: He has submitted to the king's command.' The child replied: 'Woe to you, king! Woe to you, king! If there is to be such concern for your honor, how much more concern ought there to be for the honor of God!' They arose to take him out to be slain also. Whereupon the mother said: 'Give him to me and I will kiss him first.' She said to her son: 'Go my son and tell Abraham your father: You have bound one altar, and I have bound seven altars!' " (Gittin 57).

WHEN THE CHILD BEGINS TO SPEAK

" 'And you shall teach them to your children to speak in them.' From this they (The Rabbis) deduced: 'When a child begins to speak, the father should speak the sacred tongue with him and teach him Torah. What is Torah? Rabbi Hamnuna said: 'Moses instructed us in Torah as an inheritance.' This should be the lesson of the child's first words" (Sifre Deut. and Rashi).

What is the Torah of the child? — "Moses instructed us in Torah, as an inheritance of the congregation of Jacob." Not from Moses alone have I inherited the Torah. It is an inheritance from our fathers, the whole congregation of Israel. It is not a new Torah, this Torah which I study. From the days of Moses was it given. It is not the Torah of my teacher alone, for I have inherited it from the house of my father. It is an inheritance of mine also. It is my possession. It dwells within my soul and my blood. It is engraved in my inner parts and all my limbs. This is the Torah of the Jewish child from the hour that he begins to speak.

A FIRST CONDITION: CONSISTENCY

Whatever parents teach their children, leaves an imprint upon them. But even the finest upbringing carries with it no assurance that the child will be free of failing. For the child faces many obstacles and the trials of life are many and severe. In addition to God's help, there is one factor which carries with it considerable assurance that the teachings of parents will not depart from their children in hours of temptation to wrong-doing and sin. That factor is, harmony between the verbal teachings of the parents and their own character and behavior. Their deeds must always be a shining example of what they teach their children verbally. So that, in an hour of trial, a son or a daughter might see all the teachings of their parents reflected in the very appearance of their parents' faces.

When Joseph faced the test to which the wife of his master subjected him, the teaching of his father alone did not suffice to save him from sin. The only thing which then stood by him, was the image of his father Jacob, which appeared to him at that hour. For Jacob's countenance was an utterly faithful reflection of his entire being, and his appearance could therefore instantly awaken in Joseph the total memory of all his father had ever taught him.

"And you shall teach them diligently to your children and you shall speak to them." To speak of them alone is not sufficient. Your utterance of those teachings must be reflected, "when you sit in your home, and when you walk by the way, and when you lie down and when you rise up." All your deeds at home, in the field, when you enter, and when you depart — these are to speak to your children and illustrate to them the meaning of your words.

THE MATTER DEPENDS ON FATHER AND MOTHER

Jewish tradition relates concerning the passage in the Torah on the "rebellious son" — that such an instance never occurred. It was stated in the Torah only for the purpose of inculcating a moral lesson. For, the supposition on which the image of the Torah's "rebellious son" rests, is one of total guilt on the part of the son. In actuality, most disobedient and rebellious children who turn aside from the path of probity, are victims either of faulty education or circumstances.

The primary condition for the effectiveness of parental teaching is parental example. If parents teach their children to walk in the ways of goodness and righteousness, but their own example contradicts their teaching, Scripture says of them: "Your wisdom and teaching could have been respected by your children. You yourselves have however shown that you despise its value. The fault is yours!"

"Honor your father and your mother." This mitzvah was not given to children alone. Parents are also subject to its dictate. It says to the father: before you had sons you were not bidden to accord honor to yourself, as you are now. Now that you have children, and have become a father — honor your father! That is to say, the father who is within you.

It says to the mother: Before you had children you were not under as much obligation to accord honor to yourself as you are now. Honor your mother; the mother who is within you!

There is no greater honor which a father and mother can extend to the "father" and "mother" within them, than the honor they accord to their own words, by making certain that their actions correspond to their words.

PRAYER AND EFFORT

Even if a person exerts all his strength towards the proper upbringing of his children, he still needs prayer and Divine assistance, so that blessing might rest upon his efforts. On the other hand, neither is he free even for a single hour, from the duty of personal effort and the constant evaluation of the effectiveness of his efforts.

We all owe a debt of gratitude therefore, to any one who imparts to us truthful insights and effective practical advice in the matter of raising our children.

ABSOLUTE TRUTHFULNESS

"A person ought not to say to a child, 'I will give you something and then fail to give it to the child, for the child will thereby acquire the habit of lying" (Sukkah 46).

The best education is one which is founded on truth. A person might abundantly practice mitzvoth and good deeds, but if truth is not a lamp unto his feet and he does not speak the truth in his heart, he is likened to one who builds palaces and mansions on sand. On the morrow a rain may come whose waters will wash away the foundations of the buildings, and they will completely disintegrate. Similarly, is truth the only solid foundation for the structure of a man's life. If you remove the foundation the entire structure falls. What value would be left to the entire treasured inheritance bequeathed to us by our fathers, without the foundation of truth? If we were, Heaven forbid, to find anything deceitful and untrue in the life of our fathers, could we then place trust in any of their words? For we could not distinguish between the truth and the lie in their mouths. It is only because we know that our fathers offered their lives for every jot, for every hairsbreadth of truth, that we cherish their memory and the tradition they transmitted to us. Let us then transmit to our children the teachings we wish to convey to them, exactly as our fathers taught us — without deceit. Let a boy or girl know that from the mouth of his or her parent an untruth never emerges; not in things seemingly insignificant, certainly not in money matters, and all the more certainly not in spiritual concerns. Every lie is unfit; especially is a lie unfit, if it is used as a means for conveying the truth.

The Sages permitted stretching the truth only to people of unquestioned integrity, for the sake of removing strife and enthroning peace between husband and wife, and between a man and his brother; and even then, only if there is at least a truthful aspect to what is said. To speak falsehood however to a child, ought to be avoided to the utmost. For if a child has been taught the trait of truthfulness, he has been given everything. If not, what has he been given?

EDUCATION — NOT REWARD AND PUNISHMENT

"A person ought not to discriminate between his children, for the gift which Jacob gave to Joseph made his brothers envious, and brought about the descent of our fathers into Egypt" (Sabbath 11). A father's relationship to his sons ought to be based on reason rather than sentiment.

Whether a son exhibits some superior talent or trait or grace, or is inferior to his brothers in any respect, he ought to receive equal treatment to that meted out to his other brothers. For discrimination between children leads to the harshest kind of envy.

On the other hand, if a father sees that one of his children has embarked on a path of wrongdoing and seeks to influence his other children to do likewise, then — if admonition goes unheeded, he may banish such a son from his home, so that the latter's evil should not harm his other children. (The reference is to an adult child.) And thus did Abraham do when he sent Ishmael away from his home.

Or, if a person sees that his child has some superior potential, he ought to cultivate that potential in his child. And thus did Jacob behave generally towards Joseph. When however Jacob gave Joseph a material mark of his affection which set Joseph apart from his brothers — though Jacob had all manner of justified reasons for doing so — the results were tragic. For, special attention given to a child, whether favorable or not, in the process of the child's upbringing, is proper and necessary. But the bestowal or specific marks of favor in the form of gifts or rewards of a material nature — if these discriminate between children — are improper.

"THE LEFT HAND PUSHES AWAY AND THE RIGHT HAND DRAWS CLOSE"

"It happened once that the son of Gorgos of Lud, ran away from school, and his father threatened him. Out of fear of his father, he committed suicide. It happened once that a child from Bnei Brak, broke a bottle on the Sabbath, and his father threatened him. Because of fear of his father, he committed suicide. Because of these events the Sages stated: Let not a person threaten a child with physical punishment. Let him either strike the child immediately or be silent" (Sotah 47). We learn from this that the threat of physical punishment is not a wise practice in the upbringing of a child. King Solomon said in his wisdom: "Bring up a child in accordance with his way; even when he becomes old he will not depart from it" (Proverbs 22). In other words give him the kind of upbringing which will abide in him all his life. You know that you son will one day leave your domain, and will no longer fear you. If you educate him through fear alone, the education you give him will depart from him when his fear ceases. But if you educate him with pleasantness of manner, then he will not forsake what you have taught him, even when he becomes old.

SOME GENERAL PRINCIPLES

A person ought to be careful, in feeding his children, to select only foods which are healthful, and will contribute to the perfect growth of the child's physical and mental powers.

He ought not to feed them delicacies excessively. Neither ought he to feed them coarse foods.

One ought to train his children to eat at regularly appointed times every day. They are to be taught not to eat standing, walking or lying down, but seated at the table. (There is an allusion to this in the verse: "Your children are like olive shoots — around your table.") One ought not to give them candies excessively, or stuff them with fattening foods. Their food should be tasty, served in right measure, in order that their bodies might grow up healthy and strong for the study of Torah, the service of God and the conduct of daily affairs. And thus is it said: "If a small wound is inflicted on the body — a large one results from it in the soul." Whereas a healthy body will render a person fit also for perfect spiritual development.

It is of utmost importance in the training of one's son or daughter when still small, to teach them the value of physical cleanliness, of keeping their clothing clean, and of general orderliness. Children should be taught to be careful in speech and in manners; not only towards others, but also amongst themselves. For it is a saying of the wise that the external forms of one's life exercise a powerful effect on his inner being.

Children ought to be trained to be restrained and shy towards grownups; so that they should not feel free to approach any stranger for the fulfillment of their childish wants.

Woe to people who show excessive mercy towards their children. When their children are little, they say: "Let the children have their way now, they are still small; when they grow up they will avoid evil and choose good of themselves." Such children are not likely to shed the bad habits of their childhood. Any attempt to admonish them when they reach adulthood, will be rejected by them. Therefore, parents ought to teach their children discipline from their earliest youth.

If a child does wrong, he ought not to be reminded of it excessively. He ought to be scolded at the moment, but later shown affection again. Neither should the character of his wrong-doing be exaggerated.

A person ought to indicate to his young sons and daughters the honor which accrues to the righteous. And he ought to show them the punishment and the shame which overtake the wicked. However, he ought to dwell more on the former than on the latter, for excessive dwelling on the wrong-doing of the wicked — even when done in a derogatory manner — is always dangerous; since a child is easily impressionable, even excessive criticism of wrong may have a negative effect upon him. And one can never foretell the later possible results of such impressions.

211

"It is good that a person should carry a yoke in his youth." Therefore, one ought to train his sons and daughters when they are still small, to bear the burdens of the household, even if the family is large and has many servants. It is also good to train children to show kindness towards other people and towards animals; to awaken in them sympathy for any creature in pain or trouble. Happy is the person who acquires the habit from childhood of tending to the needs of guests, of helping the poor and the troubled.

One ought to forewarn his sons and daughters when little against shaming others, against talebearing and slander. He ought never listen to them when they bear slanderous tales, and ought to scold them when they come to him bearing tales aganst one another.

RESPECT FOR PARENTS

In a home in which parents are respected, there can be proper upbringing of children. Where there is no respect for parents, there can be no proper upbringing.

Even though the Sages have said: "If a father foregoes the honor due him, his honor is forgiven" (Kiddushin 32), this is so only with reference to freedom from punishment. A father can save his son from being liable to punishment for the sin of not having honored his father, if he forgives the child. All the same the mitzvah of honoring one's father and mother is not thereby nullified, and he remains under its obligation. However, it is an unwise thing if a father too often forgives his children for failure to show him honor. For, where respect for parents is lacking, a child cannot receive a proper upbringing.

Similarly, if children see the respect given by their parents to their grandparents, they thereby learn a lesson of great value; but, if children see a lack of respect towards their grandparents, they are not likely to accord respect to their parents. At most, they will do so for as long as they derive benefit from their parents, and still remain in fear of them. When they will no longer have need of their parents' benefactions, they will treat their parents with the same disrespect the latter had accorded to their grandparents.

PARTNERS WITH GOD

In the entire Torah the commandment to accord honor to others is found only with reference to God and to parents. The

Torah does not make mention of even the honor due to a king or a sage, as an obligation. Only with reference to God and to parents does the Torah do so. In fact, God has even preceded the commandment to accord honor to parents to that concerning Himself. "Honor your father and your mother," is stated in the Ten Commandments. "Honor the Lord from your wealth," is stated in Proverbs. We learn from this that the respect due fathers and mothers is not dependent on any circumstance of wealth, wisdom, greatness or benefaction bestowed upon children. The only reason for the commandment "Honor your father and your mother," is the fact that your parents were partners with God in giving birth to you. The debt of gratitude which one owes to those who gave him life — to God and his parents, can never be completely repaid.

THE EXTENT OF THE MITZVAH

Thus did our Sages teach: "Even if one is a convert, whose father is a gentile, he is obligated to honor his father" (Maimonides).

"If one's father violated the Torah's words, one should not say to him: 'Father, you have violated the Torah.' Rather should he say: Is it written in the Torah thus and thus?' — but he should not admonish his father" (Kiddushin 32).

"Said Rabbi Abohu: 'The disciples asked Rabbi Eliezer the Great: what is the extent of the honor due parents? Said he to them, why do you ask me? Go and ask Damah the son of Netinah in Ashkelon. Damah the son of Netinah was an Ashkelonite gentile and a high ranking military officer. He once sat in the midst of men of great prominence, and his mother, who had lost her mind, struck him across the face with her shoe. He said nothing to her other than: 'it is sufficient for you, mother——,' When the shoe fell to the ground from her hand, Damah lifted it up and handed it to his mother, so that she should not be troubled. Damah never sat on a stone on which his father sat, and when his father died, he made of it an object of reverence (before which he kneeled). Once, there was lost (in the Temple) the stone of Benjamin (which was set in the breast-plate of the high Priest). It was proclaimed: 'Who is the man who has a stone like unto the original?' They said: 'Damah the son of Netinah has one like it.' They went to him and agreed to give him 100 dinar for it. He went up to the attic to bring it down, but found his father sleeping there. Some say that the key to the jewel box was placed between his father's fingers; others say that his leg was stretched out on the box. He went down to them and said: 'I cannot bring it to you now. They thought that he had changed his mind and wanted to raise the price of the gem. They raised its price to 200 dinar, to 1000 dinar. When his father woke up, he went up and brought down the precious stone and gave it to the Sages. They wanted to give him the last price they had offered, but he would not accept it. He said: 'Shall I sell my father's honor to you for money?' What reward did God give him? That night his cow gave birth to a red heifer, and the people of Israel paid him for it with its weight in gold" (Kiddushin 31; Jerusalem Talmud Peah; Deut. Rabbah).

I AND MY HOME

A Jewish person ought to look upon his home as if it were a Sanctuary, upon his children as if they were the people of the Lord, and upon himself as if he were a Kohen standing between the Lord and his people, bringing up his offerings, and drawing his children near to the Torah in order to bring them under the wings of the Divine Presence.

More than this. So great is the importance of the Torah which a father teaches his little children, that the Sages said: "Children who attend school are not to be removed from the study of Torah even for the building of the Sanctuary" (Sabbath 119). Since the Sanctuary was destroyed — the world is sustained by the breath of the mouths of school children. If, Heaven forbid, Torah ceases from the mouths of school children, the world is subject to destruction.

When the Sanctuary stood, its continued existence depended on the righteousness of the majority of the people of Israel. But a single home in which Torah and the observance of mitzvoth is inculcated, can be a foundation on which to rebuild the entire people of Israel. Therefore, the mitzvah of the upbringing of children, was given to the individual and not to the many. (Community responsibility for the upbringing of children was not made mandatory prior to the time of Joshua the son of Gamla; the obligation of upbringing children was first addressed by the Torah to each individual father.)

The commandment concerning the upbringing of one's children is stated in the first passage of the Shema — which was addressed in the singular — and which also enjoins the acceptance of the yoke of the Kingdom of Heaven. "Hear O Israel, The Lord our

God the Lord is one. And you shall love the Lord your God —
and you shall teach them diligently to your children" (Deut. 6).

Just as the acceptance of the yoke of the Kingdom of Heaven
is an individual commandment, which one is bidden to observe
even if all the world bids him do otherwise — similarly, is the
commandment to bring up one's children an individual commandment. And even if all the world were, Heaven forbid, to forsake
its faith in the Lord, let him not walk in their ways, but rather
turn to his children and his household alone, and teach them
diligently these words: "The Lord our God, the Lord is one.
His people is one — and it is sustained even by one person — I and
my household."

I and my household — this is the essence of the upbringing of
children. Teach your child this essential principle and say to him:
"You too shall be like me, my son, in submitting to the will of
the Lord of the Universe. Accept His sovereignty upon yourself,
nullify your will for the sake of His will and serve the one God
with love. In the end, everyone will nullify his will for the sake of
yours, and all will return to serve their God. And the Lord will
be King over all the earth, on that day the Lord will be one and
His name will be one!"

The mitzvah of educating one's children which rests upon the
father, is a cardinal principle of the Torah; it is the foundation
of the existence of the people of Israel and of the existence of the
world. The essence of that education is — the unity and uniqueness
of God, the unity and uniqueness of Israel, and the unity and
uniqueness of every individual son of the people of Israel.

■ UPBRINGING OF CHILDREN

1.   *Parents are obliged to train their little children in all the mitzvoth; both those prescribed in the Torah as well as those whose origin is Rabbinic. Training in the practice of mitzvoth should be given in accordance with the understanding of the child. Parents are also obliged to restrain children from anything prohibited. Especially is it important to watch over them that they speak no falsehood and utter only words of truth.*

2.   *If a father sees his child doing something improper for which he deserves punishment, he should not threaten the child with future punishment, but should mete out a penalty immediately, and subsequently show the child affection again.*

3.   *A father is obliged to teach his young child Torah, as it is said: "And you shall teach them to your children." And just as he is obligated to teach his own child, similarly is he obligated to teach his grandchild, as it is said: "And you shall make them known to your sons and to your grandsons." The son however, precedes the grandson.*

4.   *If one has not been taught by his father, he is obligated to study himself upon reaching an understanding of his obligation.*

5.   *A father is obliged to begin the instruction of his child in the Torah, when the child begins to speak. The father first teaches the child the verses: "Torah has Moses commanded us" and "Hear Oh Israel." Afterwards he gradually instructs the child in verse after verse, till the child is six or seven years old, depending on the individual child, whereupon he arranges for the child to receive proper instruction.*

6. *Every Jewish person is obligated to study the Torah; whether he be poor or rich, whether healthy or afflicted by illness, whether young or weakened by old age. Even if one is so poor that he must seek sustenance through charity, for himself and his family, he is still obligated to set aside a specified time for the study of Torah each day and each night. As it is said: "You shall dwell on it day and night."*

7. *How long does the obligation to study Torah last? — Till the day of death. As it is said: "Lest they depart from your heart all the days of your life"; and whenever one fails to study the Torah, he is subject to forgetfulness of its teachings.*

8. *"One should divide his allotted time for Torah study in three" — one-third of the time for the study of the written Torah, one-third for the study of Mishnah, and a third for the study of Gemarah, in order that he might properly understand the Torah, and that he might know what is prohibited and what permitted.*

9. *A city which has no school for the Torah instruction of children, is subject to excommunication.*

10. *The people of Israel was given three crowns to wear: the crown of Torah, the crown of priesthood, and the crown of sovereignty. Aaron merited the crown of priesthood; David merited the crown of sovereignty; the crown of Torah however, stands ready for all Israel. Whoever wishes to, may come and take it for himself. And the greatest of the three, is the crown of Torah. For it is said: "Through Me kings reign, and princes legislate righteousness."*

11. *No mitzvah is as weighty in importance as the study of Torah. Rather is the study of Torah as important as all the remaining mitzvoth together. For study leads to practice.*

12. *When Divine judgment is meted out to a person, he is judged first with reference to the extent of his engagement in the study of Torah, and only subsequently with reference to all his other deeds.*

13. *It is written in the Torah: "It (the Torah) is not in the heavens." It is not in the "heavens" — it is not found in the hearts of the haughty and the arrogant, but only*

within the humble and modest who sit in the dust at the feet of the wise. Therefore, a person ought always to cultivate, in himself and his children, the trait of modesty, in order to acquire possession of the Torah.

14. *The words of Torah do not abide with one, if he is negligent and weak willed in the study of Torah. Nor do they abide in the life of those who study Torah only when sated with material luxuries and earthly pleasures; the Torah abides only in the life of one who is willing to endure physical discomfort and inconvenience in its study. The Rabbis said: " 'If a man dies in the tent' — the Torah here teaches us allusively, that its teachings abide only in the life of one who 'deadens' himself in the tents of the wise." Assurance is given to all who study the Torah in the Beth Hamidrash (house of study) — that they will not easily forget what they learn; that all who strive in the study of Torah in modest privacy — will achieve wisdom; that whoever verbally utters the words of the text he is studying — will better remember his studies; but, that one who studies in silence — will be the more likely to forget what he learns.*

15. *It is highly praiseworthy for one to earn a livelihood from the labor of his hands. And such was the practice of the classic Saints of our people. Thereby one merits all the glory and the good of this world and the world to come. As it is said: "If you will eat the labor of your hands, happy are you and goodness is yours. Happy are you in this world; and goodness is yours in the world to come." Therefore a person is obligated to teach his son a suitable trade or occupation, from which to draw a livelihood.*

THE HONOR DUE TO PARENTS

1. *Honoring one's father and mother is a positive commandment of primary importance. Similarly does the Torah enjoin fear of parents upon us. The honor and fear due to parents is equal to that due to God Himself. It is written: "Honor your father and mother," and "Honor the Lord from yours possessions." It is written: "Each man his mother and his father you shall fear," and "The Lord your God you shall fear." Just as He commanded us to render honor and fear to His great name, similarly did He command us*

to render honor and fear to parents. And Scripture even equates the two in the matter of penalties for violation.

2. In the mitzvah of honor, the father is mentioned before the mother. Whereas in the mitzvah of fear the mother is mentioned first. We learn thereby, that both father and mother are to be accorded honor and reverence equally.

3. What is meant by fear, and what is proper honor? Fear — one should not stand or sit in his father's (or mother's place). One should not contradict his words, nor even condescendingly agree with his father's words by saying: "My father's words appear to me to be correct." One should not address his father by name in his lifetime, nor refer to his father by name even after his father's death. One should use only the title "father."

What is meant by honor? One is to serve his father and mother food and drink (for the parent's money if the latter is financially able, and for the son's money if the parent has none, but the son does). He is to accompany his parent where necessary, and serve him in all matters which are done in the service of one's master. He is to stand before him as a servant stands in the presence of his master. Our Sages relate concerning Rav Yosef that when he would hear the sound of his mother's steps coming near, he would say: "I will rise before the Divine Presence which is come."

4. If the father is a disciple of his son the father does not stand in the presence of his son, but the son stands in the presence of his father, even though the latter is his disciple. And he is obligated in all matters to place his father's needs before his own. If he goes somewhere upon his father's bidding, and others delay him on the way, he should not say: "Let me go for I have no time." He should rather say: "Let me go for the sake of my father." Similarly, should he always indicate special concern over his duty to accord fear and honor to his parent.

5. One is bidden to honor his father even after death. If he quotes him, he ought not to say merely: "Thus did father say." Rather ought he to say: "Thus did my father, my master say; may I be an atonement for him." After twelve months have elapsed from the death of his father, he ought to say: "Thus did my father, my master say; may his memory be for a blessing, for life in the world to come."

6. *Both a man and a woman are obligated concerning fearing and honoring parents; the only difference being, that the man is capable of discharging those obligations constantly, whereas a married woman is often not similarly capable because she is beholden to others. Therefore a woman who is divorced or widowed has similar obligations to those of a man.*

7. *How far does the obligation to honor one's father and mother extend? Even if they took a bag of gold coins belonging to him and cast them into the sea, he ought not to shame them, to show anger against them.*

8. *How far does the obligation to fear parents extend? Even if the son was dressed lavishly and he was presiding over a public gathering, and his father or mother came and struck him and spat upon him, he must not shame them, but must remain silent and in awe and fear before the King of Kings who thus commanded. For if a king of flesh and blood were to decree worse anguish, he could not hesitate in the matter; how much more unhesitatingly must he obey Him who created this world according to His will.*

9. *However, although we are thus commanded, a person may not excessively burden his children in the matter, lest he cause them "to stumble"; he ought not to shame them, or to show anger towards them, Rather should he be forgiving, or appear oblivious at times; for, "a father who foregoes the honor due him, his honor is forgiven."*

10. *If one strikes a grown up son, he is subject to* נידוי *(a mild form of excommunication), for he thereby transgresses the prohibition: "And before the blind you may not place an obstacle."*

11. *If one's father or mother are mentally deranged, he should treat them compassionately till they are granted Divine mercy. If however, their situation had deteriorated excessively, he should arrange that they receive the necessary care at the hand of others.*

12. *If one's father is wicked and indiscriminately trans-*

gresses the Torah's commandments, he ought not say to his father: "Father, you have transgressed the words of the Torah." Rather let him say: "Father, is such and such written in the Torah?" — as if he were asking a question of him, rather than admonishing him.

13. *If one's father bids him transgress the words of the Torah, whether with reference to a negative commandment or a positive one, or even one prescribed by our Sages, he ought not obey his father. For it is said: "Each man, his mother and father you shall fear and my Sabbaths you shall observe" — all of you are obligated to honor Me.*

14. *If one's father said to him: "Give me water," and his mother said: "Give me water," he is to bring water to his father first, because his mother and he are both obligated to honor his father. If one's mother is divorced from his father — they are both equal.*

15. *A person is obligated to honor his stepmother as long as his father is alive. He is similarly obligated towards his stepfather. For such honor is part of the honor due his own parent. One is likewise obligated to accord honor to his parents-in-law. Rabbinic prescription also enjoins one to honor his older brother.*

CHAPTER 25

■ BAR MITZVAH

■ The Torah does not impose an obligation on a child to practice mitzvoth, nor does it prescribe any punishment for his violation of them. Before he becomes an adult the mitzvoth which a child is bidden to practice are obligations on his father, not himself, for the Torah enjoins the father to train his son in the practice of mitzvoth. It is only when he becomes an adult that the Jew is held personally responsible for the performance of mitzvoth.

According to our tradition, a child becomes a man on the day he reaches his thirteenth birthday. With the appearance of stars in the sky on the first night of his fourteenth year, he is bar mitzvah — that is to say, subject to the obligation of mitzvoth. So the very first mitzvah he may perform is that of reading the evening Shema, with its appropriate injunction to accept the yoke of the kingdom of heaven.

Our sages have found support in Scripture for the oral tradition that thirteen is the age at which one begins to be obligated to practice mitzvoth. The Torah generally addresses its commandments "to the man," and no one under thirteen is designated as "man" in Scripture. (Levi is called a man at that age.)

MANHOOD AND STRENGTH

Wherever "man" is used in the Torah, it connotes strength. Judges are advised: "You shall not be afraid of the face of any man" (Deut. 1) — i.e., however powerful the man who comes before you, you shall not fear him. David urged his general Abner to feats of strength with the words: "Art not thou a valiant man, and who is like to thee in Israel?" (I Sam. 26.) A verse in Judges 8 reads: "For as the man is, so is his strength."

Now, strength is of many kinds. There is physical strength, armed with which one fears no one. There is military strength, for defensive and offensive purposes. But the greatest strength of all is inner strength, the strength a person needs in order to overcome the inclinations of his own passions. "Who is strong?" asks Ethics of the Fathers. "He who overcomes his own inclinations!" One does not acquire that strength until he becomes bar mitzvah — at the age of thirteen, if a boy, at the age of twelve, if a girl. For it is the desire of our Creator for children to be dominated by their inclinations before the onset of maturity. Whether the child does good or evil, he is ruled entirely by will and instinct. Actions motivated by will alone, and not preceded by inner spiritual struggle, are considered to spring from the inclination to evil (yetzer hara).

INCLINATION TO GOOD AND INCLINATION TO EVIL

The Jewish sages limit the inclination to good (yetzer hatov) to the strength one exerts against one's will, to one's capacity for submitting one's own will to the will and decree of the Creator. And yet, not every inner struggle, not every conquest of one's will represents a victory for the inclination to good. There are people who have no such inclination who are yet continually at war with themselves. Our instinctive desires are varied ad often contradictory; sometimes they run amock, at other times they collide with one another. There are occasions when the benficial inclinations prevail purely by accident — say, in a completely amoral person, in whom the inclination to good does not operate. So long as a person is completely free in his behavior, and has not accepted the sanction of mitzvoth, he may practice the good as a matter of personal choice rather than Divine obligation. Such a person follows his desires at all times, simply because they are his, not because they are objectively good. But when one becomes subject to the practice of commandments enjoined by the Divine

223

Power, one accepts those commandments as obligatory — and then (and only then) one's behavior may be attributed to the inclination to good.

THE VOLUNTARY AND THE OBLIGATORY

We have mentioned earlier in passing that one who does good because the Torah commands it is held by the Jewish tradition to be superior to one who does good without that sanction. Why is this so?

First, because there is no assurance of permanence and consistency in the actions of one who acts outside the Torah's sanction. He acts as the mood strikes him, in an arbitrary fashion. But one who obey's the Torah's commands, and acts in accordance with them, will so act consistently and permanently.

The Jewish people take pride in the fact that they choose to act virtuously regardless of whether that choice makes them more worthy or less (through having foregone freedom of choice), regardless of whether or not their choice is dictated by fear of punishment. Their sole intent is to make certain of the proper observance of the mitzvoth. Our superiority consists in the fact that we pursue these observances not primarily for their own benefit, but because God commanded them. It is the desire to act in accordance with the will of God which we may call "the inclination to good." We come to know this desire only after we become bar mitzvah.

A second objection to the random performance of virtuous deeds is that it accustoms one to follow his own impulsive caprices — which in the end may lead him completely astray. On the other hand, though the inclination to good does deprive us of complete freedom of choice, it at the same time habituates us to ultimate good. True, there are times when one acts out of fear of punishment, and not out of that love of God which should be one's ultimate motivation for the practice of mitzvoth. All the same, one becomes so accustomed to doing the right thing that eventually one does it with a whole heart and perfect love. For the acceptance of the obligation of mitzvoth is more important than the mitzvoth themselves, if one performs them without accepting them as mandatory.

NEW OBLIGATIONS

Immediately on becoming bar mitzvah, one is expected to behave as a man — that is to say, to use one's manly strength to overcome the inclination to evil. Fathers and teachers should assist their sons in starting their maturity in the right manner, by helping them to understand clearly the character of the new state they are entering and the obligations attached to it. The bar mitzvah must be made aware that he has newly entered into an obligation to fulfill God's commandments which he will bear for the rest of his life. The day of his bar mitzvah is as important as the day when he entered the covenant of Abraham; neither day can ever be nullified.

The bar mitzvah must have complete faith in his Creator, believing that He will give him the strength to bend his instincts to the will of his Creator.

Language is often a clue to important ideas in Jewish religious life. The Hebrew word "bar" in bar mitzvah means "son of"; the word "baal" in baal averah (wrong-doer), means "husband." Our sages have pointed out that in a certain respect the bar mitzvah is like a son, the baal averah like a husband. The Jew who practices mitzvoth becomes as permanently attached to them as a son is to his father. But he who practices wrongdoing, however frequently, can always, like a husband, *divorce* himself from that practice. The bonds of sin can be broken, but the relationship of mitzvoth becomes integral to a practicing Jew, flesh of his flesh.

THE POWER OF EVIL

This is not to minimize the power of evil. The Talmud has warned us of the danger of procrastinating in our battle against sin. "Whosoever says, I will sin and repent, sin and repent again, is not given the opportunity to repent." (Yoma 85.) We are permitted to repent only in order to be saved from sin, not as a pretext for further wrong-doing.

The power of the evil inclination resides in the variety of the forms it assumes and its persistence. It seduces us with lust; it makes black seem white, white black; it turns the wrong-doer into a misleader of others; when we feel the stirrings of repentance, it distracts us, and talks us into apathy: "You're too old to turn over a new leaf at your age." And when the wrong-doer does turn over a new leaf, the inclination to evil never lets him alone; it keeps stealing into his innermost thoughts and feelings. Without God's help, we can never overcome the inclination to evil.

It is because the battle against our evil instincts is so intense that God does not expose us to it until we have reached maturity. Children are not obligated to practice the mitzvoth and contend with their evil instincts. But at maturity, when he reaches the fullness of his powers, the Jew is sent out to fight evil — and to triumph over it.

TEPHILLIN

After the Shema, the next mitzvah a bar mitzvah can perform is a manual one — the putting on of Tephillin (phylacteries). This he does the very next morning, before he begins the day's activities.

As the recital of Shema the evening before, contained all the duties of the heart, the putting on of Tephillin symbolizes all the mitzvoth that are performed manually. The bar mitzvah who has now become a man will be distinguished by many acts of physical and spiritual strength. (Strength, as we have mentioned above, is the benchmark of manhood in the Jewish tradition.) But he must not be misled into thinking that whatever he achieves in life is to be ascribed to his personal strength. "Everyone that is proud in heart is an abomination to the Lord" (Proverbs 16). This holds even for pride that is justified — pride, that is, in virtuous action.

To escape the snare of pride, the Jew puts Tephillin on his head and arm. He is to dwell on the significance of that which is written in the Tephillin.

"And it shall be for a sign unto thee upon thy hand and for a memorial between thine eyes . . . for with a strong hand hath the Lord brought thee out of Egypt" (Exodus 13). The Tephillin are "a sign upon thy hand" signifying that it is not our outstretched hand but the Lord's that brought us out of Egypt. We are told to bind that sign on our left hand because it is the weaker one — that we may be reminded continually that the Lord alone gives us strength for valiant deeds, that His hand is present in all we do, His spirit present in all our thoughts. With this reminder we will be truly strong, truly men of valor.

BAR MITZVAH FEAST

"A good name is better than precious oil; and the day of death than the day of one's birth" (Ecclesiastes 7). The day of one's death is better than the day of one's birth — because at birth one's deeds are still unknown, at death they are known . . . Rabbi Levi said: 'Once two ships crossed at a port. As one sailed out of the harbor, the other sailed in. Everyone rejoiced over the departing ship, but there was little rejoicing over the arrival. A clever man who was there said: Things should be exactly the contrary. Why rejoice over the departing ship — her future is unknown? We ought rather to rejoice over the arriving ship: having sailed the sea in peace it has reached its destination in peace!' "

That is why it is not in the Jewish tradition to celebrate birthdays. But we do celebrate the day of bar mitzvah, for the day of one's bar mitzvah is greater than the day of one's birth. When a person is born, he is not completely fashioned. He becomes "complete" only on the day of his bar mitzvah. On that day, when he accepts the obligation of performing the mitzvoth of God, his inclination to God is firmly joined to his life, and the purpose for which God gave him life is achieved.

Two things make the bar mitzvah meal a "rejoicing of mitzvah": the bar mitzvah's utterance of words of Torah, and his being called to read from the Torah in the synagogue. The joy of the occasion is the joy of Torah, as the bar mitzvah enters into his rightful inheritance, the inheritance of Israel.

And all Israel rejoices with him.

■ BAR MITZVAH OBSERVANCE

1. *Mitzvoth are not obligatory upon a male child (in Torah law) till he has completed thirteen years of age; the age for a girl is twelve.*

2. *If a child is born on the first of Nissan, his bar mitzvah takes place on the first of Nissan of his fourteenth year, even if his thirteenth year was a leap year and therefore had thirteen months (Adar being repeated). We do not then say that since twelve months of the child's thirteenth year had passed by the first of Adar II, his bar mitzvah should take place in Adar II. We wait till the first of Nissan.*

3. *If a child is born in Adar of a regular year (which has only one Adar), and his thirteenth year is a leap year, he does not become bar mitzvah until Adar II, on the respective day of his birth.*

4. *If a child is born in Adar of a leap year, and his thirteenth year is also a leap year, his bar mitzvah takes place in the respective Adar of his birth. If the child's thirteenth year is a regular year, his bar mitzvah takes place on his birthday, whether his birth took place in Adar I or in Adar II.*

5. *If two children were born in a leap year, one at the end of Adar I, and the second, after him in the beginning of Adar II — if the year of their bar mitzvah is a regular one and has only one Adar, then the one born last will become bar mitzvah first, in the beginning of Adar; while the one born first, will become bar mitzvah later — at the end of the month.*

6. *On the Sabbath immediately preceding the bar mitzvah day it is customary for the bar mitzvah to be called to Maftir and to read the Prophetic portion prescribed for the day, but he is not called to the Torah for one of the first seven*

portions regularly read on Sabbath. For the reading of the first seven portions is an obligatory enactment prescribed by Moses (Moses prescribed public Torah reading on the Sabbath, on Mondays and Thursdays), which therefore applies only to adults, upon whom mitzvoth are obligatory. But a child before his bar mitzvah is not yet under obligation to practice the mitzvoth. Whereas the Prophetic reading is a TAKANATH CHACHAMIM (Rabbinic enactment), which was prescribed after an anti-Semitic decree forbidding public reading of the Torah.

7. *Before a boy becomes bar mitzvah he is not called to Maftir of the Sabbath of Zachor, on the Sabbath of Parah, on the seventh day of Passover, on the Festival of Shavuoth and on the Sabbath of Repentance. On those days he is called for GELILAH (the rolling up of the Torah).*

8. *On the first Monday or Thursday immediately after the bar mitzvah day a boy is called to the Torah. If the day of his bar mitzvah takes places on Friday, he is called to the Torah on the Sabbath immediately following, and he may be called to one of the first seven portions.*

9. *After completion of the portion read for the bar mitzvah, and after the bar mitzvah has recited the final blessing, his father recites the following blessing: "Blessed is He Who has freed me from the penalties due this one." There are two reasons for this blessing:* (a) *an acknowledgement of gratitude and thanksgiving to God who enabled him to raise his child in the practice of mitzvoth till the latter has reached adulthood and himself stands under the obligation of mitzvoth; so that he (the father) is now freed of the responsibility which rested upon him had he failed to properly train his son; and* (b), *an utterance of thanksgiving to God who has now freed his child from possibly being subject to penalties for his parents' wrongdoing (Yalkut Shimoni Ruth).*

A SUMMARY OF THE LAWS OF TEPHILLIN

1. *Only such Tephillin are purchased as are known to have been made and written in accord with Halachic requirements. For if they are not made in accord with those*

requirements, they are invalid for the performance of the mitzvah of Tephillin, and every blessing recited over them is for nought. Therefore it is proper to purchase Tephillin from an expert and God-fearing scribe, or from a merchant who is known to be trustworthy in the matter.

2. Tephillin which were written by one who does not believe in mitzvoth or by a child not yet under the obligation of mitzvoth are invalid and should be consigned to concealment. If they were printed and not written with proper ink or in the prescribed manner; or if any part of the preparation of the Tephillin was done by a non-Jew, or by one who does not believe in mitzvoth or by a child — they are invalid and it is forbidden to put them on.

3. The Tephillin are not to be put on before daybreak. The time for wearing the Tephillin extends from daybreak to sunset. If morning has dawned sufficiently for one to recognize a slight acquaintance of his at a distance of four elms (approximately seven feet), he may put on the Tephillin.

4. The Tallith should be put on before the Tephillin.

5. The hand Tephillin should be put on first, and before the strap is tightened on the muscle of the hand the following blessing is recited: "Blessed art Thou, o Lord our God, King of the Universe, Who sanctified us with His commandments and commanded us to put on Tephillin." The strap is then tightened, and wound seven times around the arm, and the remainder of the strap is wound on the hand. Afterwards the head Tephillin are put on and before they are tightened the following blessing is recited: "Blessed art Thou, o Lord our God, King of the Universe, Who sanctified us with His commandments and commanded the mitzvah of Tephillin." Immediately after the blessing the following is added: "Blessed be the name of His Glorious Majesty for ever and ever — and the strap is tightened around the head. Afterwards the hand strap is wound three times on the middle finger and then on the hand in such a manner that the Hebrew letter Shin is formed (Shin is the first letter of the Hebrew word for Almighty).

6. After the Service the Tephillin are removed in the

inverse order in which they are put on — first the Shin on the hand is unwound, then the head Tephillin are removed and returned to their bag, and finally the hand Tephillin are removed.

7. *The proper place for the hand Tephillin is on the muscle of the left hand. The Tephillin should be inclined towards the heart. Care should be taken that the knot in the strap, which is fashioned in the form of a Yud, should remain close to the Tephillin box.*

8. *If one is left-handed, to the extent that he uses his left hand primarily in all matters — he wears the hand Tephillin on his right hand. However, if he does some work with his right hand primarily — he places the hand Tephillin on his left hand. Similarly, if he writes with his right hand, then even if he does everything with his left hand — he places the Tephillin on his left hand.*

9. *The proper place for putting on the head Tephillin, is from the beginning of the hair line at the center of the brow till the place where an infant's skull is soft. The entire box of the head Tephillin should be placed where hair grows. The knot on the head Tephillin should be placed at the center of the rear of the head above the spine.*

10. *If the hair of one's head are long, he should take care, when he wears Tephillin, that his hair should not be combed upwards, but should remain in the direction of their growth. For otherwise they constitute "an interruption" between the Tephillin and his head.*

11. *It is forbidden to interrupt, between the putting on of the hand Tephillin and the head Tephillin, with any conversation or deed. If such an interruption has taken place, one should repeat the first Tephillin blessing when he puts on the head Tephillin; and immediately thereafter he should recite the second blessing.*

12. *If one hears KADDISH or KEDUSHAH — he should not interrupt to respond with the congregation, but he should listen and concentrate on what the congregation is saying. But if he did thus interrupt (between the putting of the hand and head Tephillin) he need not repeat the blessing.*

13. *When one takes the Tephillin out of their bag, he should take care to remove the hand Tephillin first. Therefore, one should always have some regular sign by means of which he might know where each of the Tephillin boxes is placed in their bag.*

14. *No object should be placed between the Tephillin and the flesh, both with regard to the hand Tephillin and to the head Tephillin. If one has a wound on the proper place for putting on the Tephillin, and the wound is bandaged, he should ask a competent Rabbi what procedure he is to follow.*

15. *The Tephillin boxes and the outer side of the straps, should be black and if there has been discoloration, they should be brought to an expert for blackening.*

16. *The length of the straps of the head Tephillin should reach the naval of the wearer.*

17. *One should take care that the black side of the straps shall be turned outward when he wears the Tephillin.*

18. *As long as one wears Tephillin one should not distract his attention from them. When one says, in the Shema, "And you shall bind them for a sign on your hand" he should touch the box of the hand Tephillin with his right hand. Similarly, when he says, "And they shall be for frontlets between your eyes," he should touch the box of his head Tephillin with his right hand.*

19. *When one removes his Tephillin, he should do so while standing. The Tephillin are removed first, and then the Tallith.*

20. *It is necessary to examine the writing on the Tephillin twice during every seven year period, to make certain that none of the letters were erased. At the least, Tephillin should be examined once in seven years. If Tephillin fell into water it is forbidden to put them on till their writing is examined.*

21. *Tephillin are not worn on Sabbath and Yom Tov. For Tephillin are a sign unto Israel of their relations with God. Sabbath and Yom Tov are themselves such signs. During the intermediate days of a holiday custom varies concerning*

*the wearing of Tephillin. However, in the land of Israel
the prevalent custom is not to wear Tephillin during the
intermediate days.*

22.   *Tephillin require a clean body. Our Sages said: "If
one has done his needs, has washed his hands, put on
Tephillin, read the Shema and prayed, Scripture accounts
it to him as if he had built an altar and had brought an
offering on it" (Berachoth 15).*

23.   *The sanctity of Tephillin is exceedingly great. A
person should therefore be utterly reverent when wearing
the Tephillin. While wearing them, he should not eat or
sleep. He should not hang them by their straps, nor place
them at the foot or side of the bed. He may place them at
the head of the bed. If one removes Tephillin from their
bag, and they fall to the ground from his hand, he should
fast a voluntary fast.*

*"The Rabbis have taught: Israel is beloved, for the Holy
One, Blessed is He, has surrounded them with mitzvoth —
Tephillin on their heads and their arms, Tzitzith on their
garments, and a Mezuzah on their doors. Of these David
said: Seven times daily did I praise You" (Tephillin — two,
Tzitzith — four, Mezuzah — one, equals seven. Menachoth
43).*

*"Rabbi Eliezer the son of Jacob said: whoever has Tephillin
on his head and his arm, Tzitzith on his garment and a
Mezuzah on his door — is assured that he will not sin; for it
is said: 'And the three-fold cord will not easily be severed' "
(Ibid.).*